The VIRGIN *of*
BENNINGTON

The VIRGIN *of* BENNINGTON

KATHLEEN NORRIS

RIVERHEAD BOOKS
a member of
Penguin Putnam Inc.
375 Hudson Street
New York, NY 10014

A list of permissions can be found on pages 255–256.

Library of Congress Cataloging-in-Publication Data

Norris, Kathleen, date.
The virgin of Bennington / Kathleen Norris.
p. cm.
ISBN 1-57322-179-1
1. Norris, Kathleen—Childhood and youth.   2. Norris, Kathleen—Homes and
haunts—New York (State)—New York.   3. New York (N.Y.)—Social life and
customs—20th century.   4. Bennington College—Alumni and alumnae—Biography.
5. Poets, American—20th century—Biography.   I. Title.
PS3564.O66 Z47   2001   00-053333
811'.54—dc21
[B]

Printed in the United States of America

1   3   5   7   9   10   8   6   4   2

This book is printed on acid-free paper. ∞

BOOK DESIGN BY DEBORAH KERNER

FOR DAVID

CONTENTS

But "salvation is far from sinners,"

and such was I at that time.

Yet little by little I was drawing closer to you,

although I did not know it.

—SAINT AUGUSTINE,

Confessions

The VIRGIN *of*
BENNINGTON

Chapter

One

THE VIRGIN

OF BENNINGTON

IN 1965, WHEN I WAS SEVENTEEN, I BECAME Nick Carraway. That is, I found myself living out the core of F. Scott Fitzgerald's *The Great Gatsby,* which is how young westerners adapt—or do not adapt—to what seems to them the dazzling but dangerous world of the East Coast. A middle-westerner by heritage, and far-westerner by virtue of having spent my adolescence in Hawaii, I had no idea, when I applied to Bennington College in Vermont, that I was signing up for a crash course in the turbulent dynamics of place and culture. I had chosen the school because, having dutifully fulfilled the minimum requirements for math courses at my preparatory school in Honolulu, I was seeking a place that would accept me as I was, precociously devoted to literature but unable to master the rudiments of algebra. Bennington had little in the way of a required curriculum, and I felt ready to chart my own course.

In truth, I was a sheltered adolescent from the provinces, still rooted in my family. My mother was a schoolteacher, and my father a professional musician, and I had been content to assume their interests as my own: books and music were at the center of my life. When many of my classmates were getting driver's licenses so that they could socialize with one another, I spent my evenings attending church choir practice with my parents, or accompanying my father to rehearsals of the Honolulu Symphony, where he was a cellist. Left to my own devices, I gravitated toward the periodicals room of the Hawaii State Library, or sat for hours reading in the library's pleasant outdoor courtyard.

Every morning, before I caught a school bus at six-fifteen, I would listen to portions of favorite record albums—it might be a Verdi overture, or Frank Sinatra's "Only the Lonely," any Bob Dylan song, Barber's Adagio for Strings, or if I was feeling truly moody, a solemn movement from a Bach cello suite. Listening to music was a way for me to survive another day in a school where I never felt I belonged. Many of my classmates had been together since kindergarten, and when I entered the school in seventh grade, I found a close-knit, all but impenetrable society, steeped in traditions unknown to me. Fresh from the mainland, and woefully ignorant of the complex culture of Hawaii, I was an easy target for derision.

I held on because it was an excellent school, and I learned I could take refuge in the honing of my intellectual skills, particularly in areas that did not interest my classmates. This promised me an independence I craved, and I accepted loneliness as its cost. I began to write, and also plunged headlong into existentialist philosophy. I can only wonder at the sixteen-year-old girl who went alone on a Saturday afternoon to see Ingmar Bergman's *Through a Glass, Darkly*, clutching the yellow paperback I had been reading on the bus, Søren Kierkegaard's *Fear and Trembling* and *The Sickness unto Death*. I can laugh at her now, and at the two sailors, not many years older than she, who sat behind her in the theater, growing more restless as the film progressed. They had apparently mistaken it for one of the Swedish pornographic movies then in vogue, and were impatiently waiting for the sex to begin.

My life then had direction, a straightforward goal. A steady stream of vocational, aptitude, and intelligence tests had aimed me like an arrow at college. But I was never asked to take stock of what would be required of me once I landed there, and this left me with the impression that life at college would be a continuation of what had gone before, four years in which I would read books and write papers and be rewarded by the encouragement of dedicated teachers. It never fully hit me that I would have to construct a life of my own, outside the parameters of my family. When I arrived on the Bennington campus with my parents and sisters, I was not at all prepared to watch them drive away in the Volkswagen van, en route to my father's two-year teaching stint at the Navy School of Music in Norfolk, Virginia. I could not conceive of how to proceed into the next moment, let alone an entire semester.

One of the reasons I had chosen Bennington was that, though it had a few male graduate students in dance and drama, it was a women's college, and I assumed this would allow me to study free of the distractions and social failures I had endured in a coed high school. College has long been a place where young middle-class Americans break out of the shell of adolescence. But leaping out of the provincialism of 1960s Honolulu into Bennington's aggressively au courant milieu would skew the process so badly for me that I retreated into myself for another four years. That my new Bennington friends often misread my shyness as poise, my reclusiveness as maturity only increased my sense of isolation. I felt that there was no one I could talk to about waking every morning with a crushing sense of dread, unable to bear the thought of remaining at school. College was something I had strived and longed for, and yet I felt empty there, without resources. My distant parents, the two younger sisters with whom I had squabbled fiercely in a shared room until I was well into my teens, and even my older brother, who was then with the Peace Corps in Liberia, had taken my identity with them, leaving me a shell: I was going through the motions, but was not fully alive.

I felt that I had died, and considered other people dense for not recognizing this, and for treating me as if I was still alive. One morning, in great distress, I rang the doorbell of the campus apartment of the admissions director. Finding me on her doorstep blubbering with tears, she appeared surprised that a young woman who had confidently quoted Emily Dickinson, Søren Kierkegaard, and Albert Camus in her application essay was just a homesick adolescent. She invited me in for a breakfast I could hardly eat, listened well, and then kindly advised me that the decision over whether or not to remain at school was one I might make on a trial basis every morning, in the hope that the way would be clear before me. *Can I stay here one more day? Probably. Most likely.* That became the mantra that got me through the next few months.

SPEED

What I have come to see as my quintessential Nick Carraway experience, one that replicated itself many times and in myriad ways during my time at Bennington and later, in New York City, occurred during the first class of my freshman year. I had the good fortune to have been assigned to the literature course of a poet, Ben Belitt, whose passion for literature was surpassed only by his love of teaching it. Glad to be free of the strict dress and conduct codes of my prep school, I was pleased to find that class was to be held in the common room of a dorm, and the students—nearly all of us in blue jeans—could lounge on the floor or perch on window seats.

I found a chair, and another girl took a spot on the floor nearby. Invigorated by Belitt's lecture, I was more intrigued than intimidated by the lengthy reading list he handed out. But I was distracted by my neighbor, who throughout the class chain-smoked, drank from a bottle of Coca-Cola, and ingested small white pills. When class ended, I asked her how she was feeling. She stared at me blankly, and I couldn't resist adding that I didn't think it was a good idea for her to be taking so much aspirin. She looked at me as if I were possibly the stupidest person she had ever encountered, and sneered, "This isn't aspirin, it's speed."

I was Alice down the rabbit hole, without bearings in a world that while it appeared familiar had proved unaccountably strange. Booze had been the drug of choice among my peers; even in junior high, I'd heard rumors about binge drinking on weekends, everything from beer blasts at the beach to kids' raiding the good scotch when their parents weren't home. But in the early 1960s, in our relatively gentle environs, my classmates and I were largely ignorant of drugs. It shocked us when police found marijuana at a high school in a rough neighborhood, and confirmed our suspicion that drugs were low-class. What little I knew of speed, heroin, and other hard drugs came from the newspaper, or novels such as *Naked Lunch*, which I read but barely comprehended. I had never considered that a person of my own age might be an addict.

But the girl in front of me and her addiction were undeniably real. Our encounter taught me something I had not known about myself, that like Nick Carraway, I was inclined to withhold judgment when people around me engaged in bizarre behavior. I also started to appreciate the reservations that a Bennington professor had expressed when I applied to the school. He was on sabbatical at the University of Hawaii and agreed to meet with me. After we had talked for a while, he recommended that I reconsider, and apply to a college in the Midwest or on the West Coast. His remarks had made me uneasy, but I didn't know why. I was beginning to understand.

I could not have foreseen that my four years at Bennington would be so much like Alice's journey through Wonderland, that I would often be confused or confounded by matters other girls took for granted—not only drugs, but also sex with faculty members, or their spouses, and the ministrations of psychiatrists to sort it all out. Remaining underground, as it were, retreating inward, even as I cautiously explored the peculiar landscape, seemed the only sensible response. Trying to avoid the pain of encounters I had no way of understanding, I relied on what had worked for me in high school, and spent more time with books than with other people. I often went for days not speaking to anyone.

Some girls, although they appeared bemused by my innocence, regarded it as something to be protected. Others saw me as a solid, midwestern type who could be counted on to clean up the mess after Gatsby, Daisy, Tom, and Jordan had fled the scene. Because I wasn't taking speed or LSD, I was safe company for coming down off a bad trip. Because I was still a virgin, I could be trusted with the sordid details of an abusive relationship. And if, at the end of such an affair, a friend was suicidally depressed, I would do something sensible. Heat a can of soup and sit with her in my quiet room, or tuck her into my bed and roll out a sleeping bag on the floor for myself. If a girl attempted suicide, I would walk her to the infirmary, carrying the empty bottle of pills or stanching the flow of blood until a nurse could treat the self-inflicted wounds.

But these things were yet to come. During that first semester of freshman year I proceeded timidly through my days, so overwhelmed by the challenges of college life that I was afraid to become too involved with other people. A scholarship job at the library provided my only regular social outlet outside of class, a safe environment where I could rely on a breezy efficiency to serve other students while keeping them at a distance. Given my loneliness, I was ripe for a first love affair. That it was with a young woman instead of a man had much to do with the fact that she was the first person who had demonstrated an erotic attraction to me. I'd had very few dates in high school, and several of them consisted of attending concerts with a gay musician from my father's Navy band. I was attracted to boys, but terrified when they showed interest in me. I was unconsciously drawn to this girl because she seemed less threatening to me than a man. Her manner was masculine, but her body was reassuringly like my own. Her veneer of sophistication— she owned a car, and had driven herself to college without parental assistance—impressed and attracted me, and provided a perfect foil for my out-of-placeness and naiveté. Convinced that I was in love, I used the affair as a proving ground for the emotions, an exploration of my capacity for devotion, and a testing of limits and boundaries. This is how we come to be human, after all, and learn what love requires.

But I was still too adolescent to be capable of genuine intimacy, far too absorbed in constructing my own identity. And the affair, like so many college romances, was too racked by self-consciousness to endure. What I had thought was love was, as Kierkegaard puts it in *The Diary of a Seducer,* merely the "self-love of erotic love." I can see now how comically mismatched a couple we were: she had a range of bisexual experience, while I was sexually ignorant. She had adopted the language and manner of a young tough, and I hung on to the moorings of the good midwestern girl I thought myself to be. Sexual relations were so new to me that I was far too shy and prudish to please my partner. Sadly but predictably, the affair became contentious, and we ruthlessly manipulated each other: her aggressive worldliness never quite penetrated the obtuseness that allowed me to keep my inner self well protected. I learned, of course, that love has no traffic with manipulation and insularity, and that the flames of infatuation can quickly become ashes of enmity and contempt. The histrionics that fueled our passion grew predictable and stale, and the relationship soon collapsed under its own weight.

In the emotional turmoil that accompanied the end of the affair, I turned to my parents, phoning them in tears one night to tell them everything. My mother was calm, and reacted with a comforting equanimity. My father's response was more dramatic, but equally helpful; he drove all the way from Norfolk, Virginia, to Bennington, Vermont, in a little over twelve hours, surprising me after dinner in my dorm. He had already contacted a college counselor to make sure that someone was keeping an eye on me. She had said, "We do count them, from time to time." My father and I sat for hours in a Howard Johnson's on the outskirts of town, and he related stories about himself, and his own marriage, trying to tell me that he was no expert in knowing how to do the right thing, and that when it comes to love, it is often hard to know. That night, even as I realized that it made no sense to cling to a relationship that was no more, my faith in love itself was restored. I could hope that while I was not yet ready for it, love would come in time.

Years after I had left college and the East Coast, I awoke once in the middle of the night, startled by the memory of a long-forgotten event that loomed up in a vast darkness: a small illuminated space revealed me standing in a dorm room at Bennington with my lover. It was toward the end of our relationship, when our encounters had become strained, fractious, and for me, weepy.

She had spent the afternoon driving through the Vermont countryside and had stopped at a stable to purchase a riding crop. She clearly wanted me to admire it, and take note of its fine workmanship. She insisted that I run my hands up and down the delicate leather strips crisscrossing the handle. I was bewildered by her insistence, and scandalized at the exorbitant price she told me she had paid for it. With a perfect midwestern probity that I could not have appreciated at the time, I told her I didn't know why she wanted a riding crop in the first place; she didn't have a horse—she didn't even like horses.

Sixteen years later I sat up in bed, gasping with astonishment that it had taken me so long to get the joke. And then I laughed, mostly at myself and my impenetrable denseness, which must have been frustrating to my friend. Appropriately enough, as I was living in my maternal grandparents' house, I could hear my grandmother's light, clear voice, saying decisively, "To the pure all things are pure." And I shook my head. I hadn't thought of my friend in years, and now, in circumstances I never could have imagined at Bennington—lying next to my husband in my grandparents' bed in South Dakota—I thought kindly of her, hoping that she too was laughing on that chilly autumn night, chuckling with pleasure over a good book, or roaring with gusto over something a new lover had said. I said a prayer for both of us and went back to sleep.

THE VIRGIN OF BENNINGTON

Before I arrived at Bennington, I had no notion of its reputation on the East Coast. But I soon learned that to many people the term "Bennington girl" connoted someone who was flamboyantly (if not oppressively) artsy, bohemian, and also notoriously easy with sexual favors. Once, at a party in New York City, when I was introduced as a Bennington student, another guest piped up: "Oh. The little red whorehouse on the hill." The reputation for raciness was well deserved, particularly in the randy 1960s, but was of course not the whole picture. I was by no means the only student who took her studies seriously. But I did feel isolated: my Bennington consisted of long, solitary walks in the countryside and equally long hours reading, or studying in the library. In a sense I converted the school into a cloister for myself, no mean feat when one considers the sexual maelstrom of the time.

Without meaning to, I became nunnish—quiet, withdrawn, and obviously virginal—and this sometimes made for high comedy at a place in which visiting Dartmouth boys felt free to walk up and down the halls of our dorms, hollering, "Does anyone want to screw?" Often, someone did. One of my dorm neighbors explained that sexual intercourse relaxed her if she needed a study break. But more often, a girl would call out from her room, "Why don't you go screw yourself?" In a time when most college coeds had strict curfews, Bennington students had none, and only a cursory morning check to make sure that we were alive and in our beds. This was conducted by other students, so it was easy to fudge. If a boyfriend had spent the night, or if a girl was shacked up in a local motel, having prostituted herself for a Williams boy who operated as a pimp on weekends, no alarm was raised. Students tended to protect one another's privacy, and the college refused to act in loco parentis.

In this charged atmosphere, aloofness became my shell. If I refrained from judging or condemning others, I could remain friendly but at a remove, and we could get along. This was pure Nick Carraway, a measure of self-defense mixed with a dose of denial. Yet I was learning that the distance I cultivated might be useful, and perhaps even necessary, for the art of writing. No matter how extreme the behavior of those around me, I found it interesting. It taught me what I could not have learned from books. A passage in William James's *The Varieties of Religious Experience* that had stunned me when I encountered it in a freshman literature course provided an apt description of how art was insinuating itself into my life. In a chapter on the "divided self," James quotes the playwright Alphonse Daudet commenting on the death of his brother: "My father cried out so dramatically, 'He is dead, he is dead!' While my first self wept, my second self thought, 'How truly given was that cry, how fine it would be at the theatre.'" In a similar way I observed and pondered, growing more aware of what Daudet termed a "terrible second me" that "sees into things, and . . . mocks."

I do not regret for a moment the extracurricular education that Bennington provided in human psychology and sexuality, especially in its female incarnations. For the first time I heard young women talk about how they couldn't live without a man, and was fascinated by the curious mixture of hard calculation and pitiful naiveté they demonstrated as they set about obtaining one. I watched in awe as intelligent but insecure young women sold themselves short in order to have a steady boyfriend. Often they set their caps for older, powerful men, usually Bennington professors who were all too glad to be so targeted. Several faculty members were notorious for checking out the new crop of students, and for having affairs with one girl after another. One stalked the library's all-night study room on weekends.

More than once I received an engraved invitation to an on-campus orgy; a more perfect expression of debutante wantonness could not be conceived. And when I first heard Bob Dylan's "Just Like a Woman," with its depiction of a neurotic and vulnerable young woman strung out on speed, but still wearing her pearls, it rang so true that I could have named at least five girls who fit the description. That such persistent self-destruction was possible, and among people of my own age, frightened me, and made me sad.

This was the world in which, like Alice, I had landed, to find that the mores and values I'd been raised with had been turned inside out and upside down. So much was both bewildering and illuminating to me. One weekend during my sophomore year, for example, I was looking for one of my few close friends. I knew she hadn't planned a trip home to New York City, and when I returned several times to her room to knock and call her name, I sensed that she was in there, behind the locked door. I finally saw her a few days later and learned that she had picked up a college boy on Friday night. The two of them had spent the entire weekend in bed, rousing themselves only to go to the snack bar on Saturday night for a quick meal. This behavior no longer seemed strange to me, but I did assume that it signified the start of a relationship. I made polite inquiries about the boy, his name, and where he was from. "I don't know," my friend replied. "I never asked." I was speechless. "I didn't know that you could do that," I mumbled, and it was my friend's turn to be surprised. She, like my other friends at Bennington, was puzzled by my lack of interest in sexual exploration, but generally accepted the only explanation I could give, that I simply was not ready. Our tolerance was mutual, a two-way street.

BEING POPE

The fact that I remained a virgin well into my senior year became the stuff of campus legend, complete with jokes about "Norris the Nun" and "The Virgin of Bennington." But there was no religious dimension to my situation. While I had turned my dorm room into a recluse's cell, my solitude was not holy and hospitable, but merely a means of retreating from other people and their demands. It had none of the self-giving that a true religious vocation requires. As yet, I had not enough self to give. "Formation" is the term monastic communities use for the period in which novice monks and nuns are guided and trained, before they make their solemn vows. I happened to undergo my formation not within convent walls but in the wilds of Bennington in the late 1960s.

I never did feel quite at home at Bennington, although I came to love the place and am grateful for the education I received there, both in human nature and in the art of literature. The college set me on the path of becoming a writer. But emotionally, it was always a difficult place for me. Like Nick Carraway, I discovered that my habit of reserving judgment had "opened up many curious natures to me," and made me privy to other people's secrets; I became something of a confessor, or at the least, a repository of other people's stories.

Late in my junior year my peculiar role at Bennington was acknowledged by the other girls in my dorm in a manner that combined girlish whimsy with uncanny prescience. At our first Sunday-night social of the spring semester, we decided to designate titles and roles for the upperclassmen. We chose a Terpsichore, an Artist, a Scribe. My friend Andrea Dworkin was declared our Oracle, and a charming, boyish homosexual girl was named Knight Errant. I spoke up and said that I wanted to be the Poet, but someone misheard me and declared me Pope. I protested, but to no avail.

I was annoyed and more than a little baffled. I had been raised a Protestant, and hadn't been to church since arriving at Bennington. I was Pope nonetheless, and I had my duties. On Sunday nights I would enter the dorm's common room with my face powdered white, and gray shadow under my eyes to make me look unworldly, burdened with the care of souls. For a vestment I wore a floor-length Mother Hubbard muumuu with a high neck and long sleeves. And because a Pope needs a scripture, I read aloud from my facsimile edition of *Alice in Wonderland*. This is what passed for liturgy at Bennington College in 1968, when having any sort of campus ministry program would have been unthinkable. Our religions were the arts and psychology. And as silly as our schoolgirl nicknames and Sunday-

night rituals were, they gave us a small measure of communal identity that, in turn, made us feel more at home.

Although I could not have imagined this then, my years at
Bennington did constitute a sort of priestly training. I had to learn to
listen carefully, without rushing to judgment. The primary education, or formation, if you will, that I received in college had little to
do with books and everything to do with mercy. I learned that sexual preferences and practices, no matter how depraved they might
appear on the surface, were significant only insofar as they affected
who a person became. Controlling and manipulative sex would
replicate itself in controlling and manipulative behavior in the classroom or with one's friends. Wantonness might be sheer desperation,
masking a suicidal self-debasement, but it might also represent a
joyful, lusty sexuality that indicated, at heart, a vast generosity of
spirit. Sexual abstinence might be wise and thoughtful, or an embit-
tering rage that fed on belittling others for their perceived sexual
weakness. Even as my own sexual experience remained extremely
limited, I gained a broad perspective on the range of human sexuality that has served me well.

I now recognize that having friends who indulged in sexual
behavior that I found incomprehensible was a test of my spirit that
would have been familiar to fourth-century Christian monks. They
were uncannily wise about the strength of human sexual desires and
blasé when fellow monks would succumb to temptation. The real
scandal, to them, was in assuming that such behavior would cut a
person off from God. Despair, loathing, and presuming to judge
were far worse than any sexual misconduct: if the erring monk were
to indulge in self-hatred to such a degree that he began to feel that
his prayers for forgiveness were useless, or if other monks con-

demned and rejected him for his licentious behavior. The literature of early monasticism sometimes shocks with its absolute refusal to judge other people. It insists on the supreme value of being steadfast in loving others.

I regret the times when I was not steadfast, when I withdrew from friends in need. One classmate, when she learned she was pregnant, returned from the doctor's office in a manic state. Angrily grabbing my arm, she said that I couldn't imagine how terrible it was to have something growing inside and not be able to stop it. To her, the pregnancy was no more than a cancerous tumor, and she hit herself repeatedly in the abdomen with her fists, as if she could make it go away. After asking me to phone her psychiatrist in New York City, since she was too distraught, she told me, wearily, that she had been seeing a psychiatrist since she was twelve, and seemed annoyed that this amazed me. I dialed the number for her, and once I had determined that he was making arrangements for her to fly to the city to have an abortion—this was in the days when a legal abortion took place only after a panel of psychiatrists attested that a woman was too mentally unstable to undergo a pregnancy—I went to the library and stayed there for hours. I could not face her anger, her suicidal craziness, and the profound sadness of the circumstances. I have always been grateful that she did not kill herself that day, and ashamed of myself for having abandoned her.

One reason I tended not to judge others at Bennington in terms of their sexual mores was that I had determined that my abstinence did not spring from any excess of virtue on my part. In my mind, at least—and I was resolutely cerebral in my college years—I thought I might be as promiscuous as many of the girls around me. In fact, it was years before I could see a connection between sexual activity and morality. And by that I mean nothing narrow-minded, but as large as love: the rightness of treating people, including one-self, with respect, honor, and trust, preparing the earth of the heart in which love can grow. At eighteen, I thought it only a matter of time before I would "fall in love," and of course, I would know it was really love, and then the fulfillment of sexual intercourse would follow.

FALLING

I was still wading cautiously on the shores of life, willing to get my feet wet but not venture into the depths. When I finally took that step, it was every bit as misguided as my earlier schoolgirl romance. An older man, one of my professors, seemed exciting yet safe, less demanding than a boy of my own age might be. The professor was married, which I unconsciously interpreted as meaning that I could have all the thrill of a romantic involvement without being asked for a genuine commitment. I was relieved to find that his marriage appeared solid, and that I liked his wife. It was years before I could admit how badly I betrayed her. At the time I wanted to believe that I was so insignificant as to be almost invisible, and that I would be able to have my affair with her husband without leaving any effect on her, or their marriage.

This denial eased my sense of wrong, and for a time the affair buoyed me, stimulating me not only sexually but intellectually as well. I was discovering a whole new self. Any discriminating person might have seen that I was simply in love with love, and a spicy, forbidden love at that. I was just young enough to be devastated when, after I had graduated and moved to New York City, I learned that the man was a habitual philanderer, and was already trading me in for a younger model. His brusque dismissal, with a shrug and a terse "You knew this wouldn't last," was both contemptuous and pleading: he was hoping that I'd be sophisticated enough to exit quietly, and not make trouble.

My lover's words were truer than I wanted to admit. Deep down, I had known that an adulterous student-professor romance was not destined to endure. And as painful as his rejection was, it also had a salutory, bracing effect: a burden whose weight I had greatly underestimated had been lifted, and my life was again my own. Dimly, through my anguish, I could recognize liberation: I was free, but adrift, as untethered as a runaway balloon. I left his apartment and made my way up West End Avenue as if learning to walk again. The experience gave me the title for my first book of poems, *Falling Off.* I felt that I had come to the end of the world, and might indeed fall off. Yet the moment was unaccountably full of promise, and even joy.

I will always regard it as an example of God's great mercy and inexhaustible creativity that so unpromising a creature might begin to turn her life to the good. And not only that: the very things that had gotten me into such irredeemable messes were the instruments of my conversion. It was the illusion of love, for instance, that drew me to New York City. I would not have had the fortitude to move there on my own had I not been energized by the folly of romance. And my philandering professor had done me a good turn by setting up a job interview for me at the Academy of American Poets, where I worked during the winter term of my senior year at Bennington, and where I returned after graduation. The woman I was to work for over the next five years proved to be a mentor who would introduce me to the idea of writing as a genuine vocation, and teach me that it was possible for a writer to, in one of her favorite phrases, "live by her wits." And this, in time, would help me summon the courage to move to my ancestral ground in South Dakota and try my hand at freelancing. These are the sorts of connections and transformations that work their way through any life. But this is my story, and it begins with an untidy but cheerful job interview on a snowy day in early December 1968.

Chapter

T w o

WORLDS

❧

WHEN ELIZABETH KRAY DIED, IN 1987, THE poet Stanley Kunitz was quoted in *The New York Times* as saying, "With her unique mixture of idealism and common sense, she was the moving spirit behind most of the programs and activities that have made New York the poetry capital of the United States, and an international poetry center." At her funeral he said simply that American poets had lost one of the best friends they ever had.

Near the end of 1968, when I interviewed with Betty for a job at the Academy of American Poets, I knew nothing of her long-standing friendships with many of the poets I had encountered in high school textbooks: Auden, Cummings, Moore. I was unaware that since the mid-1950s Betty had also been a behind-the-scenes promoter of many of the younger poets I had read in high school and college—Galway Kinnell, Denise Levertov, Richard Wilbur—or that she had initiated Andrei Voznesensky's first American tour just a few years earlier. I knew only that I wanted to be in New York City because the teacher I had a crush on—it had not yet blossomed into an affair—was based there. And a job that would require me to attend poetry readings several times a week was my idea of heaven on earth.

The interview was scheduled during the few days I'd planned to be in New York en route to a Christmas vacation with my grandparents in South Dakota. I was surprised to discover that despite its grand title, the offices of the Academy consisted of a few dusty uncarpeted rooms in a nondescript five-story building on Madison Avenue between a Gristede's supermarket and the elite Frank E. Campbell funeral home. (It has long since been replaced by a gleaming high-rise condominium.) Betty's den was cramped, and agreeably cluttered. As she swept books and papers from a faded lumpy armchair so that I could sit down, I glanced around the room. Having grown accustomed to the disdain urban easterners so often manifested toward the rest of America, dismissing it as "flyover country," I was pleased to see that a large map of the United States dominated one wall, a miscellany of ephemera affixed to its borders with thumbtacks.

In our initial small-talk, mostly about my studies at Bennington, I revealed that I would be flying to South Dakota the next day. Miss Kray perked up, as if I had finally said something of interest. "Where?" she asked, and I explained that my grandparents lived in a tiny town in the northwest region of the state. "Where, exactly?" she insisted, and I rose and shuffled some books to get closer to the map. I pointed to Bismarck, North Dakota, then as now site of the nearest commercial airport, and traced the 130 miles or so of two-lane blacktop leading south and west to Lemmon, South Dakota, where my mother had grown up and I had spent my childhood summers.

Betty questioned me intently about my grandparents, and about my ties to South Dakota, which at twenty-one I considered tenuous at best. Then she told me, proudly, that she was also a westerner, from Seattle. She mentioned that one of her forebears was a surveyor and engineer who helped map the Continental Divide. She also told me I had the job.

I thought it prudent to mention, because she had not asked, that I was a reasonably fast and accurate typist, and that my scholarship jobs in prep school and college libraries had acquainted me with what was then the ultimate in office equipment, the IBM Selectric typewriter. Miss Kray nodded in a distracted fashion, as if to say that she had assumed as much. Many years later, she told me that her sole purpose in interviewing me had been to determine if I was overbearingly arty, a stereotypical "Bennington girl." But my plainspoken, girlish manner, my sensible snow boots and practical clothing—corduroy slacks and a lamb's-wool sweater from a mill store in Vermont—led her to believe that I might be trusted with such mundane tasks as typing, filing, and running errands to the post office and bank. My having roots in South Dakota clinched the deal. After Christmas, I would return to New York and spend the college's two-month nonresident term working at the Academy.

In 1969 the Academy was impressively matriarchal. Its founder, Marie Bullock, lived a few blocks away, in a Fifth Avenue penthouse, and I sometimes was asked to deliver her daily packet of correspondence. (The doormen came to know me, but they so scrupulously observed the proprieties that one day, when I appeared eating an ice cream cone, they frostily directed me to the service elevator instead of the one I customarily took, which opened directly into the foyer of the apartment.) Mrs. Bullock's story appealed to me. Having grown up in France, the daughter of a socially prominent financier, Marie Bullock had been distressed, on moving to the United States, to find that poets here were accorded little respect and even less remuneration. She conceived of the Academy when Joseph Auslander, the professor in a class she was attending at Columbia, explained that the poet he had invited to read from his work could not take leave from his job at a soda fountain. After consulting with poets and businesspeople, and with a boldness befitting a twenty-three-year-old, she founded the Academy of American Poets in 1934, during the midst of the Depression, and ran it from her apartment for the next twenty-five years.

Her goal was to build an endowment for an annual poetry fellowship, the first of its kind in America. The initial award went to Edwin Markham, followed by Edgar Lee Masters. In democratic America, Mrs. Bullock did not want to duplicate the Académie Française; she intended that the chancellors of the Academy represent the various regions of the country, and also that the institution be supported by a broad membership of poetry lovers. Early donations were small; in an interview she recalled that her young daughters loved the adventure of opening the mail to see how much was enclosed, usually a dollar, sometimes five, with an occasional, and much-exclaimed-over, ten.

Marie Bullock's husband, Hugh, was an investment banker with a distinguished pedigree. His late father, Calvin Bullock, was a pioneer in mutual funds, and by the late 1950s his firm, Calvin Bullock, Ltd., considered on Wall Street the Tiffany of the mutual fund business, was the largest such company in New York City. With her husband's connections, Mrs. Bullock could prevail on the captains of industry to "make a sound investment in beauty" on behalf of American poets. By the time I arrived at the Academy, she had convinced both Thomas Watson, Jr., of IBM, and Mrs. Arthur C. Burns, whose husband was then a leading economic advisor to the president, to serve as officers on the Academy's board of directors.

By 1959, after she had established an annual fellowship, a publication award for a first book, and college poetry prizes nationwide, Marie Bullock knew that the Academy needed office space and an increased staff. In 1962 she hired Betty Kray as the Academy's first executive director. The invitation came at a good time for Betty, who had recently resigned from her job as director of the poetry program at Manhattan's 92nd Street YMHA. She received permission from the Rockefeller Foundation to bring to the Academy two of her programs that the Foundation had funded in the 1950s, a reading series presenting young, unknown poets, and a network of regional poetry-reading circuits that gave poets throughout the country an opportunity to expand their audience. Likewise, Betty brought along a grant she had received from the Bollingen Foundation in 1960 to commission some fifty American poets to translate their contemporaries from around the world. Betty hoped that Mrs. Bullock would be a valuable ally in helping her fund new programs, and in 1964, when she began to imagine sending poets into New York City classrooms, she was pleased that Marie Bullock enlisted U.S. Steel as a sponsor for the first artists-in-schools program in the nation. Betty Kray once credited Mrs. Bullock for taking a businesslike approach to the support of artists, and thereby helping smash the stereotype that poets had to do with "pink teas and silly women."

Originally hired at the YMHA Poetry Center in 1954 as a director of special projects—a job she once described to an interviewer as "agitating for younger poets"—Betty by 1956 had obtained grants to augment the Center's big-name readings (T. S. Eliot, Dylan Thomas, Robert Graves) with a series she called "Introductions." It presented young poets—Paul Blackburn, Robert Bly, Robert Creeley, Carolyn Kizer, Kenneth Koch, Anne Sexton, William Stafford among them—many of whom were not yet published in book form. Donald Hall recalled later that his 1956 appearance with Alastair Reid and May Swenson was his "second or third reading ever, certainly [his] first in New York." When she moved to the Academy, Betty inaugurated an annual reading series that included as its premiere event Sir John Gielgud reading the poems of T. S. Eliot, who had been scheduled to appear but had become ill. Later John Berryman gave what is believed to be the first public reading from *The Dream Songs*.

I picked up this history in bits and pieces while working at the Academy. Every time I stopped to admire a poet's photograph on the wall, or the dramatic poster that Mrs. Bullock had commissioned for her first major fund-raiser, a "Poetry Ball" held at the Waldorf-Astoria in 1935, illustrated with a muse who seemed a combination of Athena and Joan of Arc, someone would start telling stories, filling me in. The Academy's staff then consisted of two mature women with a long tenure, and a young married woman, a novelist whose husband was finishing a Ph.D. in literature. She and I had in common the fact that we had both been scholarship students at expensive schools, she at Sarah Lawrence, I at Bennington. I was replacing one of the "college girls," young women like me who tended to work at the Academy for a short time before moving on.

I had no idea how long I would remain. I had found New York frightening when I first encountered it as a Bennington freshman—too fast, too large, too noisy, too full of people. Honolulu had been a small town by comparison, and the sense of urban anonymity was vaguely threatening. For most of my time at Bennington I rarely ventured to New York, even with college friends who were from the city, but by late in my senior year I was keeping assignations with my professor in borrowed apartments in Manhattan. Our affair had started during my nonresident term, and was in full force that spring, a dizzy season in which I was infatuated with him, with poetry, and with what I thought was love.

After graduating from Bennington, I spent the summer of 1969 at home with my family in Honolulu, scarcely believing that in a few months I would be living in New York. My mother and I were both apprehensive, but the more she expressed her concerns the more determined I was to keep my fears to myself. My move to the city in the fall was eased by friends through whom I found loft- and cat-sitting opportunities to tide me over until I could find a place of my own. After a harrowing apartment hunt—scary neighborhoods, dark and grimy apartments, peculiar landlords, gruff realtors—I ended up rooming with a college friend in a small apartment on West End Avenue, a penthouse that had been tacked onto the roof of a prewar building. My starting salary at the Academy was $115 a week, and the apartment rented for the princely sum of $375 a month. But it was sunny, with a view of the sky, and a small terrace where I tried, without much luck, to grow cherry tomatoes.

Although I felt certain I had acquired a worldly air, I must have seemed impossibly young to the other women at the Academy. When I was going through Betty Kray's papers after her death, I found that she had saved a Valentine I had made for her out of construction paper, paste, and dime-store rickrack. I had given such cards to all four women in the office, and it must have been obvious to them that I was attempting to make of them a family, replicating a life I needed to outgrow. Over time, the women did become for me a covey of mothers, each very different from my own, thousands of miles away in Honolulu.

Mrs. Elbridge Gerry III, a widow, was Mrs. Bullock's assistant and the Academy's bookkeeper. Ellie was among the most fascinating people I had ever met, and was for me the ultimate New Yorker, able to reminisce about a childhood in a brownstone on Fifty-second before it became a commercial street, teeming with what she called "those dreadful speakeasies," not excluding the legendary '21' club. Ellie was so thoroughly acclimated to the city that she far preferred the predictable landscape of concrete to the vaunted glories of nature. Once she complained of relatives north of the city who had invited her for a fall weekend: "All they want to do is drive around and look at the damn trees."

Ellie balanced her cynicism with good humor. When she would discourse on money and marriage—subjects closely related in her mind—I sometimes felt that I had stepped into a novel by Dickens or George Eliot, in which the potential unions of young people "in society" are brokered like business mergers. Ellie seemed to have mixed feelings about having married well, in terms of social status. The first Elbridge Gerry had been a signer of the Declaration of Independence and served as vice-president under James Madison. But Ellie took her listing in New York's Social Register with a grain of salt, and resented the strained financial circumstances that had forced her to work well into her sixties. "I'm not as proper as I pretend to be," she told the writer Susan Mernit, who first encountered the Academy as a teenager enrolled in one of its workshops and later came to work in the office. Ellie then launched into a racy story of a long-ago picnic at City Island, complete with martinis on the beach.

While Ellie was full of puzzling admonitions—when I used

the adjective "gorgeous," she snapped, "Wherever did you learn that word?" It's common"—the gentle attentions of the Academy's membership secretary, Dorothy Ampagoomian, were more comprehensible to me. A bright and capable woman with a high school education, she was concerned that I not make too much of my book learning, or the literary reputations of the poets who visited the office. Dorothy had her ways of determining whether or not they were worthy of her attention. A willingness to talk about their children or to share recipes earned her respect.

I was terribly ungrounded then, almost as cerebral as my poetry. Having to cook for myself on a tight budget had slimmed me down, too much so in Dorothy's watchful eyes. She looked for ways to feed me, not only with home-cooked dishes that she sometimes brought from her kitchen in Yonkers, but also with stories about her youth and marriage, in what was an attempt to guide a flighty young woman along the right path. These tales emphasized the importance of family, discipline, hard work, and self-respect. Dorothy was earnest and unsophisticated where Ellie was sarcastic and urbane. I adored them both.

And no doubt I needed their ministrations. I had little idea of how to manage the tasks of daily life. When confronted with the challenge of feeding myself, I adopted a routine of shopping once a week for boxes of frozen vegetables, and a pound of ground sirloin which, after working in a few spices, I would form into individual patties and freeze. Most nights I would eat a hamburger, soggy vegetables, and boiled rice, splurging on fresh fruit or ice cream for dessert. When a friend gave me a simple recipe for a sauce for the meat, I regarded it as a great advance. But when I took the unprecedented step of inviting a friend to dinner, I had to beg for recipes from everyone in the office until I had a menu within my capabilities. My life in the city seemed a kind of fiction to me. I had never imagined living in Manhattan, although at fifteen, having discovered *The New Yorker* in the Hawaii State Library reading rooms, I had begged my parents for a subscription. While many of the cartoons were beyond me, and the advertisements for "hand-made Belgian shoes" were coded messages from an alternative universe, I nourished myself on Joseph Mitchell, John Updike, and Janet Flanner.

When I did move to New York, I was afraid much of the time, overwhelmed by ordinary chores such as shopping for clothes or groceries. Not until I read Joan Didion's essay on her move to the city, "Goodbye to All That," did I realize that my experience was not unique. Didion might have been speaking of me when she wrote: "I was in a curious position in New York: it never occurred to me that I was living a real life there." I would lurch abruptly from days of terror, when I was too anxious to leave my apartment, to days of great possibility, when all things were open to me, and Manhattan (and therefore the world) was in the palm of my hand.

My first city home was a large loft in Chinatown that a college friend, a dancer, offered to share with me. He was tending plants and cats in lieu of paying rent in a building on East Broadway, across the street from a sweatshop whose fluorescent lights made the loft's living room glow dimly all night. My worried parents in Honolulu sounded reassured when I told them that I was seldom alone in the evenings; I would often come home from work to find the loft owner's troupe of dancers stretching or rehearsing in the large mirrored studio.

When I did have to provide for my own apartment, even the thought of purchasing salt and pepper shakers filled me with trepidation. They seemed too real, too concrete, too adult. And when my roommate insisted that we needed an Oriental rug for our small living room, I was dazzled to think that we could select it, have it delivered, and call it ours. But even this lovely and useful object was fraught with more responsibility than I could bear. When my roommate and I went our own ways two years later, I was relieved that her mother wanted the rug. I was glad to get out with just a trunk full of books and clothes, and my typewriter, the small cast-iron model my mother had used at Northwestern in the 1930s.

My job at the Academy allowed me to retreat from the pressures of having to create a life for myself. There, I could hide my terrors behind a mask of efficiency, relying on skills that had served me well in school: prioritizing tasks, writing, typing. But I approached the job timidly, and was reluctant during my first week even to answer the telephone. One day Dorothy forced me into it. Glaring at me with eyebrows raised, she silently willed me to pick up a ringing phone. Over a static-riddled line I heard a growl that might have been a "Hello," and then four words slowly enunciated in a gravelly tone: "This is Mr. Auden." He wished to speak with Betty, but I managed to cut him off. I later learned that he had been at a pay phone in Mineola, Long Island, where he was participating in an Academy-sponsored in-service course for public school teachers, and had used his last coins to make the call. It was an appropriate beginning for me at the Academy: I had nowhere to go but up.

OLD MONEY

One of the strangest things about the Academy was that the office followed the holiday schedule of the New York Stock Exchange, which did not include Columbus Day or Veterans Day. Wall Street was the center of the Bullocks' world, and the Academy had been drawn in by centripetal force. The Academy's bank, for example, was the Morgan, and occasionally it fell to me to take a hung-over, sleepy, and thoroughly scruffy poet into the stately branch on Madison Avenue so that he could cash the hundred-dollar check for his reading the night before. The cool, preternaturally calm interior of the bank fascinated me. I knew nothing then of "personal banking," but I recognized the quietly luxurious and assured atmosphere that speaks of great wealth.

Because of the Bullocks' highly placed financial and social connections, the tiny organization always had access to top-notch firms. Doremus & Company, a marketing and communications agency serving the financial industry, handled the Academy's few press releases, such as the announcement of the annual fellowship or the Lamont Poetry award (now the James Laughlin Prize). The brochure for the annual reading series was printed by the prestigious Bowne company, founded in 1775, and now the world's largest financial printer. The first time I delivered copy for the series to the Bowne offices on Hudson Street, at the industrial edge of the West Village, I stared at the labels for premium liquors displayed on the walls, which indicated that Bowne's usual order ran to millions, not the few thousand leaflets the Academy required. Still I was treated with deference, reminded once again that the Academy, small as it was, had powerful connections in corporate America.

Several times a year I was dispatched from the Olympian heights of poetry to the dark canyons of the financial district. I would grab a few dollars in petty cash for a taxicab—a rare treat, as I ran most of my errands on foot or by subway—and feel very important as I sped down the FDR Drive with papers for the Academy's attorney at One Wall Street. And once a year Wall Street sent emissaries to us, in the form of auditors from the accounting firm of Lybrand, Ross Brothers, and Montgomery. Being assigned to the Academy was apparently a trial-by-fire for apprentice accountants, and the young men in their starched shirts—they were all men in those days—always seemed terrified at first. Our office had the look of a college all-night study room, and there were no men present, only the faint specter of Calvin Bullock, Ltd. But each year, as the accountants settled in, their unease would turn to gratitude when they found that our account books, reflecting individual donations as well as grants from corporations and governmental arts agencies, were in good order. They never relaxed enough to share our hot-plate lunches, however, and gravitated toward a lunch counter down the street, where they ate with undertakers from the Campbell funeral home.

Perhaps the real purpose of any "first job" is to teach us what we want, and don't want, out of life. The Bullocks' world was new to me, and I did not know how to read the signs of old money: their listing in the Social Register; the penthouse at 1030 Fifth Avenue, where they had lived for many years; the summer home on Martha's Vineyard; the winter residence in Hobe Sound, Florida. When I first visited their apartment, I was startled to see a photograph of Queen Elizabeth and Prince Philip on the grand piano, and even more startled to read the inscription to "dear Marie and Hugh." I later learned that during a visit to Washington, D.C., in 1957, the Queen had bestowed on Mr. Bullock an honorary knighthood, the first such investiture performed by a British monarch on American soil.

In a narrow hallway lined with family photographs, I found one image so familiar to me that I exclaimed aloud: there, in the middle of Manhattan, was the stately Royal Hawaiian in Waikiki, in a picture taken not long after it opened in 1927, when as one of only two hotels on the beach it was still the exclusive province of Hollywood royalty and blue-book socialites. Mrs. Bullock seemed pleased that I recognized the friend who had posed impishly with her on the sand, the actress Marie Dressler. On another occasion, when I admired the antique leather bindings of a set of books in her formal living room, Mrs. Bullock opened the glass doors of the cabinet and allowed me to examine volumes that had come from the library of Queen Marie-Thérèse of France. They had been a gift to Mrs. Bullock from her husband.

The fortune that could sustain such a gesture was incomprehensibly immense, and I realized it was nothing I wanted. Over the years I knew the Bullocks, I came to be more impressed by their devotion to each other than by their wealth, which they took for granted. There were comical moments in our relationship, minor collisions between disparate lives. Every winter Mrs. Bullock shopped at Bonwit Teller for Christmas presents for the Academy staff, and her gifts were thoughtful: I still wear a necklace of gold-wire coils and a winter scarf that she gave me. One year I received a cotton shift in a print very much like that of an inexpensive Indian bedspread I'd had in college. Such dresses sold for a few dollars then in the Village or near Columbia University; I hated to imagine what one cost at Bonwit Teller. All the women in the office received boxes of nylon stockings until 1970, when Ellie Gerry explained to Mrs. Bullock that young women were no longer wearing hose and garters. She reported this conversation to us, relishing the fact that Mrs. Bullock had not yet heard of panty hose. We received boxes of panty hose after that.

When we learned from Ellie that the Bullocks were celebrating a milestone wedding anniversary, Dorothy and I collected a small sum from everyone on the staff and went shopping in Yorkville, a neighborhood east of the Academy, and put together a box of imported fruit juices. The Bullocks were so touched by our gift that it surprised me, until Dorothy said, "I don't think the rich are used to having people give them things." Every Christmas the Bullocks did receive a slew of ugly corporate gifts—I recall a throw pillow in bristly fake fur—some of which they pawned off on the office.

B I G   C I T Y

I came to work for Betty at a time when she was focusing the Academy's resources in New York City's public libraries and parks. She had recently completed her work with a pilot program she had begun in 1965, using grants from the Rockefeller Foundation and other private charities as seed money to send a group of young poets including David Antin, Kathleen Fraser, and Ishmael Reed into forty-seven of the city's eighty-nine high schools, beginning in February 1966. Later that year Betty obtained the first literary grant from the recently established National Endowment for the Arts, which enabled her to initiate similar programs in Chicago, Detroit, Minneapolis, Pittsburgh, Tucson, and Los Angeles. By the time I arrived, these activities were running independently of the Academy, which could not sustain them once the original grants ran out. Betty's being a born instigator suited the Academy's limited resources, and it suited her nature to initiate a program, generate interest in it, and then let go. In 1970, when the NEA proposed that the state arts councils springing up across the nation take over and expand her poets-in-schools program, Betty was ready to move on.

This proved a windfall for me, as my job gave me an incomparable introduction to the many diverse worlds that constituted New York City, from the rarefied atmosphere of the Morgan Library, where the Academy held an annual reading by noted poets such as Robert Lowell, to beleaguered public libraries in the city's poorest neighborhoods, where the Academy sent writers to give readings and conduct writing workshops for children and teenagers. I had a vivid experience of the Academy's wide reach one fall day in 1971 when Betty and I took the subway to the South Bronx and toured the area with local librarians who were helping us set up programs at the Mott Haven and Tremont branch libraries. As we walked past block after block of abandoned buildings, the librarians informed us that many of their patrons, working families with children, lived in such derelict surroundings. These parents, who often worked two or three minimum-wage jobs each to make ends meet, and used the libraries as refuges for their "latch-key children," would welcome any after-school programs we could offer. That evening, I put on my best dress and presented a talk on the parks and libraries program at the Academy's annual meeting, held, as always, at the elegant Colony Club on Park Avenue.

I felt privileged to be a witness to the whole of New York, top, bottom, and in between, and even now, more than twenty-five years after moving to the western Plains, I retain a strong affection for the city. Many of my college friends had landed jobs in Manhattan, but I was one of the few whose work took her to all five boroughs. When Betty obtained her first grant from the City of New York to put on poetry readings in public parks, I was sent to promote the events within each neighborhood. I had to talk with local librarians and approach businesspeople about putting up posters or distributing flyers.

I would descend into the subway at a familiar location in Manhattan, then surface in the Bronx, or Queens, or Brooklyn, feeling like an explorer for whom everything in sight is new. I delighted in the magnificent tree-lined boulevards of Brooklyn, the great expanse of Prospect Park, the delicious scents that permeated the garden for the blind at the Brooklyn Botanic Garden. And in my travels I learned to tell when a neighborhood was in decline. On one chilly spring afternoon, I went directly from one such community, the sad and nearly deserted streets of Brooklyn's Sunset Park, to a thriving neighborhood in Flatbush, whose small-town feel recalled the Great Plains towns I knew from childhood summers.

At one bakery, the staff indignantly refused to let me leave my flyers, even though I pointed out that the poet who would be reading lived in the neighborhood. Coming from a cultural institution in Manhattan, I might as well have been from Mars. This was my introduction to the deeply rooted neighborhood chauvinism that fuels New York's provincialism. My husband, who grew up in a northern suburb, told me that on his first day at a Jesuit high school open to boys from the entire metropolitan area, he found that many of his classmates from the Bronx, Queens, and Brooklyn had never before been in Manhattan. They thought him odd because he had favorite places in all the city's boroughs, including Staten Island.

When someone told Betty of a massive weeping beech tree in Flushing, Queens, she insisted that we take the subway out to have a look. The tree turned out to be on the grounds of an old Quaker meetinghouse that before the Civil War had been a stop on the Underground Railroad. Inspired by this history, Betty set about to arrange one of her "tree walks" there. These were events held in city parks led by a naturalist and a poet, who would alternate talks on the natural world of the park with readings of poems appropriate to the setting. On many of these walks, new trees were planted.

Working with city libraries provided other opportunities to experience a New York very different from the insular world of literary

Manhattan. In helping us find sites for poetry programs on Staten Island, librarians there gave Betty and me a tour that encompassed sleepy fishing villages and one leafy town that looked as if it had been magically transported from New England, a white church steeple being the tallest structure. The librarians told us that one of New York City's last commercial farms, in New Springville, had only recently closed, a victim of industrial pollution and rising real estate values.

Through the contacts the Academy was developing with city librarians, I became better attuned to the great diversity of New York, and learned where the most recent groups of immigrants were settling. Haitians, for example, were moving into areas around Brooklyn's Prospect Park and on Manhattan's Upper West Side, and through community teachers, priests, and block organizations we were able to find a Haitian poetry and music troupe to perform in parks in both neighborhoods. But Flushing came to symbolize the immigrant process in New York for me, containing a more concentrated and energetic ethnic diversity than anything I had seen in Manhattan. When we were planning a reading series at a branch library there, the librarians informed us that the clientele included elderly Jews and Irish, young Hispanic families, and an increasing number of Chinese and Indians, both Sikhs and Hindus. This was in 1971, but a recent *New York Times* article reported that the Flushing branch library is now the busiest branch in a system that is the busiest in the nation. It is still renowned for its ability to adapt to and serve each new immigrant group that settles in the neighborhood, and it currently carries books in forty of the hundred languages spoken by Queens residents.

The Business of Art

I happened to come to the Academy at a time of great literary ferment in America. Small presses and lively new journals were emerging, and Fran McCullough at Harper & Row was bringing out first books by poets of my generation, including Gregory Orr and James Welch. It seemed a good time to be a poet. New grants and awards for writers were being offered, and institutions of a kind that had not existed before—the Coordinating Council of Little Magazines, Teachers & Writers Collaborative, and Poets & Writers, now the preeminent service organization for America's professional writers—were appearing on the literary landscape.

The world of arts administration was still very small in the early 1960s, funded by private money and populated largely by the likes of Marie Bullock and Betty Kray, whose vocations had arisen out of a simple desire to foster poets and their poetry. They had few credentials, and what they did was not yet regarded as a profession, with degree programs offering certification. The public money that would pour into state arts councils and the NEA in the late 1960s and 1970s, expanding arts programming beyond anyone's expectations, was still on the horizon.

Galen Williams, the energetic young woman who in 1962 moved into the position Betty Kray had vacated as director of the YMHA Poetry Center, began receiving small sums from the New York State Council on the Arts in 1966, to supplement the fees poets received for readings. By 1970, John Hightower, director of the Council, was encouraging her to think in bigger terms, to go after larger grants then becoming available. She founded Poets & Writers with a grant of just $5,000, and within two years was able to receive six times that amount. Funding was suddenly there for anyone who could come up with intelligent programs, and as Galen once told me, people started to run with it, and it looked as if there was no end in sight.

At the Academy, as we continued to administer the annual fellowship and develop our reading series and awards programs, we also found ourselves immersed in grant-writing for new projects. But we had little sense of direction, and a freewheeling spirit prevailed. We had no development director, and not even the thought of hiring one. We wrote no "mission statements" and did no long-range strategic planning. Ideas that came up during Betty's conversations with a poet would materialize as a grant proposal and grow into an Academy program for which I happily did the grunt work. Elizabeth Bishop's enthusiasm for the poetry of Brazil, where she maintained a home, led Betty to obtain funding so that the Academy could commission a number of American poets to translate Brazilian poetry into English. The book that resulted, edited by Bishop and a Brazilian writer, Emanuel Brasil, and published by Wesleyan University Press in 1972, was the first extensive volume of twentieth-century Brazilian poetry in English, and is typical of an Academy project in that others used it as a springboard for further work in the field. One of the poet-translators, William Jay Smith, and Brasil edited a subsequent anthology of younger Brazilian poets.

Betty's desire to collaborate with other New York City institutions pointed the Academy in a number of directions. With the Museum of the City of New York we presented Julio Marzan offering a bilingual reading and discussion of the works of three Hispanic Caribbean poets, Julia de Burgos, Pedro Mir, and Luis Pales Martes, and with Asia House we hosted a symposium featuring American writers and three Japanese poets whom we had invited for a nation-wide tour.

The Academy's programs in public libraries evolved into Saturday-afternoon writing workshops for teenagers in three Manhattan neighborhoods and in the South Bronx. And funds from the city Department of Parks and Recreation allowed the Academy to present a three-year series of outdoor readings. In Bryant Park, the backyard of the New York Public Library at Forty-second Street, the venerable Mark Van Doren gave one of his last public readings, and in a program honoring the Objectivist Press, Charles Reznikoff read his own poems and the poet Harvey Shapiro presented and discussed the work of Louis Zukofsky. At City Hall Park we held a tribute to Marianne Moore, with readings from her work by several poets and Michael Burke, then president of the New York Yankees. Betty wrote to Elizabeth Bishop that while Burke "read like a schoolboy, [he] looked superb and told an anecdote that I like. When the Yankees invited her to throw out the first ball of the opening season, Miss Moore thought she must literally pitch it from the mound, and one winter's day, with snow still on the baseball diamond, she appeared at the Yankee offices in the stadium and asked if she might practice."

In the summer of 1971, after I had won a manuscript competition for a first book of poems, Betty allowed me to read in Bryant Park with four other young poets, Erica Jong, Gregory Orr, and Bill Zavatsky, who were students in the Columbia University writing program, and Gerard Malanga, who was well known in New York for his appearance in Andy Warhol movies and a cameo in which he helped provide a suitably degenerate background for the acclaimed Hollywood film *Midnight Cowboy*.

Erica's first book of poems, *Fruits & Vegetables*, had just appeared, and her publisher had arranged for her to have a book party at a fruit-and-vegetable stand. This event gained coverage on local television news, an unheard-of accomplishment for a book of poetry. Erica told the audience in Bryant Park that as a girl she had kissed the photographs of authors on the backs of book jackets, wanting to be an author herself one day. Her raw yet focused ambition made me feel like a kid wobbling around in her mom's high heels. Poetry had been like dress-up for me, and while it was becoming more important in my life, I was unsure of what that could mean.

Chapter

Three

HOW TO BE

A POET

I FELT LUCKY TO HAVE FOUND THE IDEAL JOB in New York. If I budgeted carefully, it provided me with just enough to live on, and it also legitimized my interest in poetry, allowing me to transpose it from the realm of study into the workaday world. The job was formative in many ways, primarily in acquainting me with people who demonstrated that it was indeed possible to pursue writing as a vocation.

Many of the poets who passed through the office and read on the Academy series were college professors. But I had no desire to teach, and was fascinated by poets who had not taken up an academic career. Betty Kray encouraged me in this, telling me of May Swenson, who had for years been a legal secretary, keeping her poetry largely a secret from her colleagues at work. And of Hayden

Carruth, who had a small acreage in northern Vermont and did odd jobs—carpentry, hauling, some farm labor. When I was helping Betty arrange the first American tour for the Swedish poet Tomas Tranströmer, we were interested to learn that he was a psychologist specializing in adolescents, and people recovering from severe trauma. He told us that one of his young patients, upon escaping from a prison for juvenile offenders, had traveled through Sweden using as his alias the poet's name. Tranströmer took this dubious honor in stride.

In college I had not felt compelled to decide what I wanted to do with my life, other than continue to read as much as possible. If pressed, I mentioned that I might obtain a degree in library science, which seemed a safe course. Instead, as if on a dare, I chose to go to New York, responding to experiences at Bennington that had awakened a nascent sense of myself as a writer.

That I had begun writing poetry in earnest during my freshman year had in itself been a surprise. And it would not have happened but for the encouragement of my teacher, the poet Ben Belitt. When I arrived in his class I was still treating poetry in the manner that had earned me respectable grades in high school, as a problem to be solved using intellectual means. My pitiless dissection of a graceful lyric by Thomas Traherne had greatly amused Belitt, who said poetry was my bête noire. But my response to one writing assignment he gave—to write a description of a person using no adjectives—led him to suggest that I try my hand at verse. And once I started, I never looked back. I read and wrote poems as if my life depended on it.

Poetry became so important to me that I opted to participate in a literary competition rather than attend one of the massive demonstrations against the Vietnam War that flooded Washington,

D.C., with students from colleges along the East Coast. Some people at Bennington reproached me for this, but my friend and dorm-mate Andrea Dworkin supported me in my decision, understanding that it was my choice to make. As a high school student living in military housing near Pearl Harbor, with neighbors in Navy intelligence, I had been aware of the escalating American presence in Vietnam before it became a feature of the nightly television news. At Bennington, I had participated in silent vigils organized by local Quakers, but in the spring of 1969, when I learned that I had been named a finalist in a competition for college poets, the Glascock Contest, I felt that I had to see it through. While my schoolmates were reserving seats on chartered buses that would take them to Washington, I bought my ticket for a solitary Trailways trip from Bennington to Mount Holyoke College in Hadley, Massachusetts, where I would read with the other contestants. I spent the long day of travel wondering if the panel of judges, Louise Bogan, Stanley Kunitz, and James Merrill, would be as intimidating as I feared.

The three poets were most gracious, and at a party after the reading, Louise Bogan sipped scotch and entertained the rapt audience with stories about T. S. Eliot. She told us that he had unforgettable eyes, like a cat's. Her own lively blue eyes intrigued me. I was having so much fun that I didn't mind in the least learning that I had tied for second place with David Lehman, an undergraduate at Columbia. First prize went to a young man who has not been heard from since. Years later, I read that Bogan had described him in a letter to a friend as "a hippy boy" writing "gutsy stuff," while I was "a Bennington girl [who] was also good, [who had written] a poem to her stomach (as distinguished from her uterus)"—a wry reference to a recent poem by Anne Sexton that Bogan disliked. She had enjoyed the event at Mount Holyoke, and commented that she had

enthusiastic about writing; he had lately begun to feel that he was all written out, and had been forced to consider the possibility that he had nothing more to say. (Fortunately for him, and for lovers of poetry, he was to be proved wrong.) I didn't know how to reply, except to keep listening as he gave voice to his anxieties. I was deeply touched that he would reveal so much of himself to me. In doing so he helped me put poetry in a new perspective; it was more than a passion to get words on paper, it appeared to be a way of life.

THE ANGEL HANDBOOK

But what kind of life? At Bennington, I had steeped myself in the Romantic poets, which meant becoming immersed in heady notions of the poet as mystic, seer, lover, hierophant, drunk, and all-around screw-up, an identity just foolhardy enough to attract me at the time. I was writing papers that I intended to work up into a senior thesis—critical essays on Mallarmé and Rimbaud, Coleridge and Baudelaire, and Keats's *The Fall of Hyperion*. But I also wanted to include in the thesis a collection of my own poems, and brief prose reflections on such diverse subjects as religion and aesthetics, symbolic art, poetic consciousness in the songs of Bob Dylan and Randy Newman, and more humbly, the joys of laundering and singing. Gradually, my own writing became for me the most important part of the thesis, and I entitled the whole mess after one of the poems in it, "Excerpts from the Angel Handbook."

This poem plunged me more wholly into the process of writing than anything I had previously done, and also was a significant factor in my decision to move to New York. Ironically, it was fear of the city that had inspired me to write it. During the spring of 1969, as graduation approached, I decided to compose a kind of memo from heaven, a guide for angels who found themselves stationed in Manhattan. It began as a flippant catalogue of advice:

Be careful how you unfold your wings—
there are some in the world who are not content
unless their teeth are full of feathers

You may find employment with the Sanitation Department
or at any laundry

When you cross at intersections look both ways, then up

Bits of my past began to surface. I played with the math anxiety that had vexed me since third grade, when long division stumped me:

Their logic will not make sense to you,
their mathematics especially will be impossible,
for you will never be able to divide anything

The poem took a more serious turn, becoming a meditation on the nature of love:

You will never tell a lie,
but you will have many secrets

You will meet some whose faces give a glow
as if they once had halos:
these are the lovers,
you will make a lot of love

I concluded the poem with a verse intended to assure me that New York would be survivable, after all. It might be a dangerous city, but I would find it a place suffused with angelic presence:

> *. . . your flights, even though you are careful*
> *to keep them invisible, will make those who love you sad:*
> *they will not understand that you never go anyplace*
> *you're not meant to be.*

I became so thoroughly absorbed in the writing of this poem that it acted like the light in an incubator, drawing me out of my shell. Uncharacteristically, I started to talk about what I was writing, and shared lines from the handbook with people who knew New York City far better than I. One day I mentioned the poem over coffee in the Bennington Commons, and the lone professor in the group, who had recently obtained a Ph.D. in literature from Columbia, said, dismissively, that I couldn't possibly write a poem on the subject of angels without first reading several books, whose titles he then began to list. I surprised myself by saying, firmly, "No. First I have to write the poem, and then I will look at the books." I was not trying to be fatuous, though I'm sure I sounded that way. I had obviously annoyed the professor. But I didn't mind, because the world had just opened up for me: I had identified an essential difference between the poet and the scholar, and knew for certain which ground to claim as mine.

Another event during my senior year that formed me as a poet was a reading by Michael Dennis Browne, a British writer whose first job in America was teaching for a year at Bennington. He read his own poetry and generously shared the work of a contemporary, James Wright, whose poems from *The Branch Will Not Break* and especially his newest book, *Shall We Gather at the River*, shook me to the core. Over the past few years I had studied poets I could admire but not hope to emulate—everyone from the seventeenth-century metaphysicals John Cleveland and John Donne to twentieth-century giants such as T. S. Eliot and Ezra Pound. I had learned a great deal about what was good in these poets and others, but had never encountered work that said to me so clearly, *I want to write like that.*

Browne explained that after having hit bottom in his life—a descent into alcoholism and the subsequent loss of his job and family—James Wright abandoned the formal and florid style that had won him accolades as a young man, and stripped down his prosody so that the poetry became both more simple and more emotionally intense. This combination appealed to me, and after Browne's reading I bought Wright's books and read them over and over.

Once I had moved on to the Academy, I was thrilled to meet Wright, a friend of Betty Kray. He was one of the young poets she had sent on reading circuits in the late 1950s, and in 1965, during the bleakest part of his life, she had suggested that he move from Minnesota, the scene of his recent personal disasters, to the East. "So many people would want to put themselves out for you," she wrote him, "that you really could move from one household to another." She offered him a room in her apartment while he looked for a job. The letter was a lifeline, and Wright, anticipating themes that were to haunt his poetry, wrote to thank Betty for her "overwhelmingly beautiful letter.... Enough of brooding ... I'm sick of dying. Where to live—I prefer to die elsewhere than Minneapolis." He sent Betty some of the poems that would inspire me in college, and she replied: "I like the poems, Jim. I thought about poetry when I was forking garbage into my compost heap. Out of the compost comes wonderfully textured, clean, beneficial humus and yet, my God, what this end product requires! Dung, garbage, worms, ashes!"

James Wright did move east, and both he and his poetry rose from the ashes. When I met him, he had recently married his beloved Annie, an elementary school teacher, and was teaching literature at Hunter College. I relished the fact that this most bold and ardent poet was cleverly disguised in the rotund body and modest demeanor of a midwestern banker. The Academy staff came to treasure his phone calls: I—or whoever answered—would be treated to an enthusiastic recitation of some poem or other, not one of his, but the work of another poet he felt compelled to share. Whatever he had been reading, perhaps a new translation of Georg Trakl or Pablo Neruda sent to him by his friend Robert Bly. I remember getting a flood of Goethe in German, and when I commented that I didn't know German, Wright said it did not matter, as I could still hear the beauty of the sound. And it was true.

Wright knew an alarming amount of Whitman by heart, and once, when I accompanied him to an Academy program in Queens, he gleefully recited what he termed, with great affection, "bad Walt." His booming voice unsettled the other riders in the subway car, but when they saw me laughing, they relaxed. I'm sure they wondered, though, about a grown man in a business suit who would loudly declaim:

> *A tenor large and fresh as the creation fills me,*
> *The orbic flex of his mouth is pouring and filling me full.*
>
> *I hear the train'd soprano (what work with hers is this?)*
> *The orchestra whirls me wider than Uranus flies,*

It wrenches such ardors from me I did not know I possess'd
  them. . . .
Steep'd amid honey'd morphine, my windpipe throttled in fakes of
  death,
At length let up again to feel the puzzle of puzzles,
And that we call Being.

What Every Young Poet Dreams Of

Possibly the best thing that the Academy of American Poets did for me was to provide an opportunity to attend poetry readings, night after night, for close to five years. I was doubly fortunate, for Betty Kray was, as many have acknowledged, one of several people who were instrumental in popularizing the poetry reading in this country. The poet John Malcolm Brinnin was another, for his urging Dylan Thomas to tour the country beginning in 1950, and then accompanying him on the road. Betty Kray's work was behind the scenes, as she wanted it; in a 1959 Voice of America interview celebrating the twenty-first anniversary of the YMHA Poetry Center, Betty downplayed her role as executive director by stating with typical modesty that it amounted to the tedious task of "solving all immediate problems."

But poets knew better. William Jay Smith wrote in a brief memoir of Betty that when he first met her he knew she was "the kind of person every young poet dreams of. There were not many poetry readings, and certainly no poetry circuits in those days, and university lecture committees . . . turned to [her] for advice and assistance." Most colleges wanted only the stars who would guarantee an audience, but Betty "saw to it they took the lesser-known poets as well. . . . I was one of many who benefited from her careful attention."

Donald Hall has stated that Betty was "a little-credited source of the growth of the poetry reading, which has been the most astonishing change in American poetry in my lifetime." In his book *Poetry and Ambition*, he writes that she "instituted statewide poetry circuits . . . in which colleges combined to share travel expenses as a poet hurtled from campus to campus; each college paid the poet a small fee—a hundred dollars, mostly—but volume enabled a young poet to clear in two weeks a useful sum." Betty told me that she had seized on the idea of circuits in the early 1950s as a means of standardizing poets' fees. It was a simple way to benefit both poets and the colleges, which by cutting expenses for each poet could afford to sponsor more readings.

By the early 1960s Betty had accumulated a list of contacts for her circuits that included Paul Engle and Donald Justice in Iowa, Leslie Fiedler in Montana, Isabella Gardner and James Wright in Minnesota, Thom Gunn in California, Daniel Hoffman in Pennsylvania, Edwin Honig in Rhode Island, Judson Jerome in Ohio, Theodore Roethke in Washington, Karl Shapiro in Nebraska, W. D. Snodgrass in Michigan, John Tagliabue in Maine, Allen Tate in Wisconsin, and Richard Wilbur in Connecticut. Some writers welcomed the circuit readings for the opportunity to get out of town. Louis Simpson, who was then teaching at Berkeley, observes, "Though writing was a private affair, I did not want an isolated life. So I started giving poetry readings. I flew to Oregon, Minnesota, Michigan, Pennsylvania, Tennessee, New York. Most of these readings were arranged by the Academy of American Poets. You gave an hour's reading of your poems, and went to a party, and the next morning were sent flying on your way or were driven to the next town. This was known as a circuit."

In his memoir *North of Jamaica*, Simpson connects the vitality of the poetry in postwar America with the craze for readings. "At the beginning of the 1950's Dylan Thomas burst on the American scene, bringing with him a new concept—at least it seemed new at the time—of poetry as the spoken rather than the written word." This was the idea to which Betty Kray was to devote herself: recognizing that poetry is an oral art, not a mind game played on paper. She believed it was a living, breathing voice asking to be heard, and for more than thirty years she found ways to make it heard. The atmosphere for readings was distinctly chilly when she started sending well-known poets such as Stephen Spender and Edith Sitwell on American tours. Colleges then did not expect poets to read from their own work, but preferred them to give public lectures.

That tepid and faintly damning term "arts administrator" can't begin to describe the zest with which Betty translated a love for poets and poetry into a vocation. Stanley Kunitz admitted that before meeting her in the 1950s, when she was at the YMHA, he had expected "a self-serving bureaucratic type with literary airs," and instead found "someone who was down-to-earth, generous, buoyant, and simply mad about poetry." The two worked together on most of Betty's projects from then on, cofounding Poets House in 1985.

When I met Betty, a generation after Donald Hall, William Jay Smith, and others had been encouraged by her, she was still very much the sort of advocate "every young poet dreams of." And her commitment to poetry as an oral art had, if anything, strengthened over the years. Betty had been a pioneer in using bilingual readings to introduce American audiences to poetry in foreign languages, and at the YMHA and later at the Academy, she presented the work of such poets as C. P. Cavafy, Giuseppe Ungaretti, Jorge Guillén, George Seferis, Saint-John Perse, and Octavio Paz. "With the bilingual readings," she said, "I fiercely fought to have the English read first, and then the foreign poem," believing that listeners would be more alert to the beauty of the original when they had some sense of the form and meaning of the poem. "The translation will remain in their minds," she maintained, "but the Spanish poem, the real poem, will remain in their ears." This arrangement was unheard of at the time, but the enthusiastic response of audiences confirmed Betty's insight.

For me, Betty's trust in the oral quality of poetry, and the experience of readings at the Academy and elsewhere in Manhattan, cleared my head of the notion I had fallen for in school: that poetry is mostly a matter of profound ideas crammed into loaded words, a puzzle to be solved by pulling apart and analyzing the words. Listening to a poem is a far better approach to understanding, for hearing a poem is an experience that begins with words and, if all goes well, ends in silent assent, and even wonder. The ideas are there, but submerged, inextricable from the whole. Except in very bad sectarian verse, they are never the point.

In my time at the Academy, I heard many fine readings, some mediocre ones, and a few that were truly terrible, demonstrations of ego in which a poet, seeming to forget that others were present, would retreat behind a lectern and drone on for thirty minutes, poem after poem, without break or change of inflection. After one such reading, Betty observed that in her experience, the upper range of people's ability to concentrate on listening to poetry was twenty minutes. She left me with two principles on which I have based my own readings: that the poet must avoid using the occasion to inflict the maximum number of poems on an audience, and that it is always better to leave people less than sated, wanting more.

I'd had little opportunity to read my work in public, just enough to be terrified at the prospect when, in 1970, I won a slot in the YMHA's "Discovery" reading series for young poets. Betty made me practice with a tape recorder, and while it helped, it made me even more self-conscious, so that at my reading, I uttered the words in a hoarse whisper, trying to remember to pace myself and not swallow the ends of my lines. I'm sure I sounded like a drunk who overcompensates by speaking much too slowly. Afterward one superattenuated intellectual declared that I had invented a whole new reading style. When I discovered that he was not being facetious, I said that it was nothing of the kind: I had simply been nervous.

A reading by Denise Levertov was for me a seminar in how to do it right. I was thrilled to hear a poet I had found on my own in high school. Her *O Taste and See* was one of the books—Allen Ginsberg's *Howl* was another—that I would carry in my bookbag to read during long waits for the city bus that would take me from my high school or the Hawaii State Library to Navy housing at Pearl Harbor. Poetry and music were my lifelines during adolescence; I once claimed to have found "the key to everything" in the Shirelles' *Greatest Hits* album. Thus I could readily identify with the girls in Levertov's "The Secret," who tell her they have found the secret of life in one of her poems, but not what it is, or what line it is in. That was how I approached poetry then, hungrily, as if it held the answers to the questions that raged within. Poetry constituted survival.

Levertov's style of reading—natural, yet with a dignified pace and tone—made me aware that my own shyness was a form of pride, one I would have to shed if I were to communicate effectively with an audience. But more than that, Levertov gave me a sense of what a poetry reading could be. As was the custom, she had been paired that evening with another, younger poet, whose first book had garnered some attention. This poet prefaced each poem with a lengthy explication that made the poem, when it finally came, appear superfluous. Either her ideas about the poem had not been realized in the work itself, or her off-the-cuff stories were livelier than the poetic versions. She seemed self-satisfied, unaware that her work came across as clever but shallow. It reminded me uncomfortably of my own writing, which I sensed had more brittle wit than substance. The performance left me feeling exhausted, and a little depressed.

And then Levertov took the stage. By the time she finished one poem, I felt as if I had been refreshed by a glass of cool water. To employ a phrase Betty sometimes used to explain why people go to poetry readings, it was the relief of hearing language again after so much verbiage. No clever surfaces here, but only words that mattered, words with authority. No longer did I feel merely a passive witness to a poet's vanity. Levertov brought the world in, and allowed me in as well, and the darkened auditorium became a sacred space, a place of prayer and meditation. She made me aware that a poetry reading could be an act of generosity to an audience, to which anyone might respond with the whole heart.

Listening to Levertov was inspiring, even though she forced me to face the deficiencies in my own verse. I was being reminded that I was not yet a poet, but as had happened when I first read the poems of James Wright, I was being shown a direction in which to go.

K N O C K - K N O C K

A major part of my job at the Academy consisted of making arrangements for poetry readings and arriving early in order to welcome the poet and the introducer, and show them the auditorium at the Guggenheim Museum or the Donnell Library where the readings would be held. Betty insisted on sound tests. And she instructed me to lie: the more nervous and out-of-sorts poets appeared, the more effective I must be in convincing them that they seemed very calm under the circumstances.

Betty was always better at that than I, but I learned a great deal by watching her. Once, when we had gathered two poets who were to read, one of them, who was currently fashionable in New York, announced to the other, who was making his first appearance in the city, that she had better read second, since the audience was coming to hear her. If she went first, she explained, people might leave when she was done. Betty, detecting the anger rising in me, said, "We won't let them behave like that." The poet, realizing her gaffe, said, "Oh. My analyst tells me that I'm very tactless."

Before I could offer a resounding agreement, Betty invented a pretext to separate the poets, and sent me to the empty auditorium to help the rattled out-of-towner recover. I asked him to go to the mike and read a poem. He read a few lines in a strangled voice, then stopped. I asked him to tell me the silliest joke he knew, and he responded with a knock-knock joke. I countered with one of my own—the Existentialist Knock-Knock Joke, which the other person has to start. He fell for it, and it made him laugh. Then I asked him to read another poem, and this time his voice was stronger. I complimented him on his diction, and he relaxed. The reading went well, and afterward Betty reminded me that it was our job to get both poets in shape to read, even if one of them was acting like a jerk. "They were both nervous, you know," she said, "but one of them had an unfortunate way of expressing it. And I hope you realize that she thought that by invoking her analyst, she was making an apology. I believe it's the only apology she's capable of." I was speechless, but wiser.

A quality that William Jay Smith said he had admired in Betty Kray was her desire to have every poet's reading be worthy of the effort she knew had gone into the poetry. This was due to her love of poetry and poets, and also to the fact that Betty's husband, Vladimir Ussachevsky, was a composer; she had long conceived of a poetry reading as comparable to a musical performance, and as such, something that should be staged. Her friend E. E. Cummings shared this view, and in the early 1950s had often complained to Betty about the haphazard onstage arrangements he encountered on the road: scratchy microphones or none, wobbly lecterns under poor lighting, which made it difficult for him to read.

Betty said that Cummings had immediately taken to her because she had instinctively done what he felt should be done to stage a reading of his at the YMHA. When, in 1954, he hired Betty to act as his agent for reading tours, the two concocted a set of "stage directions" that became notorious among college English departments. Although these might appear simple enough, they were sometimes resented, mocked, and resisted. Cummings requested an armchair, a small table, and a goose-necked lamp, and begged off any obligation to attend a dinner with college faculty before the reading. Marianne Moore, another poet for whom Betty sometimes arranged readings, preferred a lectern, with an extra table for her books alongside.

As Betty herself wrote, college English departments in the 1950s *had a bad reputation among poets. Each poet had a store of favorite horror stories. Marianne Moore's had to do with a cocktail party given in her honor by a faculty member who had a three-legged dog. He and the dog (she liked the dog) met her at the train and took her to his home where the party was going strong. When the time approached for her reading, nobody seemed interested. She sneaked herself into the dining room, barricaded herself behind several chairs, and changed her clothes. . . . Then she found somebody willing to drive her to the university, where students were waiting [for her] in a crowded room.*

At another of Moore's readings, some careless person had placed the book table at a distance from the lectern. Every time the seventy-three-year-old poet wished to read from another book, she had to walk back and forth across the stage. The program had begun inauspiciously, with an introduction by a man Betty described as "a stupid professor of creative verse, a so-called poet enamoured of himself," who cited at length "adverse criticisms of [Moore's] poetry, obviously intending to refute them by resoundingly delivering his own estimate. But unfortunately his triumphant vindication collapsed in a muddle of feeble remarks; the voices of her critics were stronger than his." When she dared to look at Moore during this awful recital, Betty found her staring straight ahead, her face flushed. Betty noted with admiration that Moore managed to make "a whole cloth of this chaotic program—the trips to the table, the slippery arrangement of books and papers"—so that "it all came out right."

THE SHELLEY DISEASE

In strict terms, my job at the Academy was mostly drudgery. Typing, filing, sealing and stamping envelopes (ever mindful of Mrs. Bullock's stipulation that stamps be neatly aligned with the upper right-hand corner), and running errands that included what must have amounted to weeks of standing in line at the Gracie Station post office. Yet in all of this, I was learning from Betty Kray how to be a poet. A real one, not a pseudo-Romantic suffering from what Louise Bogan termed "the Shelley disease," using the name of "poet" to excuse selfish and boorish behavior. From my perch at the Academy I witnessed plenty of behavior that was boorish and worse, and it made me aware of how heavily I myself had invested in the notion of the artist as solitary genius, more "sensitive" or "creative" than lesser mortals. This pose had served me well in high school and college, as insulation from the rejection of my peers, and protection for my shaky self-image.

It was also a trap. Like many adolescents, I had taken up writing poetry in self-defense, hoping it would provide protective coloration. This is a common experience, but can imprison the poet and cause the novice to believe that the best writing, or the only writing, comes when one is most depressed. For years I labored under that dangerous and self-imposed limitation, and I was not helped by knowing that a number of the contemporary poets I had imbibed in college—Sylvia Plath, Delmore Schwartz, James Wright—had been tormented by alcoholism, madness, or suicidal impulse. It was almost as if self-destruction had become for poets an occupational hazard.

I needed someone to steer me in another direction. And I found that person in Betty Kray, who knew very well the vulnerability of poets in a culture that despised their work as vague, sentimental, and irrelevant, and at the same time asked them to fulfill the priestly role of descending into the depths and returning to speak of it. Betty never discounted the pain—she spoke matter-of-factly about a friend who had told her she had started drinking as a way to come down after the ecstasy of writing, and now had to struggle to get her life back—but she also maintained that poets must be practical, as they must make their own way in the world.

My study of literature in college had allowed me to idealize the poet as someone who seeks out the highs in life, despising what is ordinary, so Betty's attitude was a welcome tonic. She approved of my ability to live on my salary—which eventually was raised to $150 a week—and the discipline I mustered to put anything extra, such as baby-sitting income, or the rare fee for a reading or publication, into a savings account. She convinced me that my competent, managerial side need not interfere with my other, more creative abilities.

I think of Betty as my first reader, of both my life and my art. She knew what to make of the poems I was writing in my twenties, poems so inward, so masked, that thirty years after having written them, I no longer know what I was trying to say. There's an odd, urgent hunger in them, a searching for something I could not yet name, the sense of being on the verge of enormous upheaval and change. But the language is inarticulate, knotted, locked up, as if written in code. Betty was the mentor, the force, who helped me break the code, allowing both me and my poetry to emerge.

I must have been a curious girl then, needing mentors to point out the obvious. Even my first book seemed a fluke. I happened to mention to Betty's good friend the poet Jane Cooper that I had been accumulating a great pile of poems and had noticed that my new work was thematically related to earlier poems, including some I had written in college. She suggested that what I had might not be merely a stack of poems, but a book. Her comment was like a lightning strike in my life, an unexpected affirmation of my vocation. Without it, I doubt I would have had the courage to enter a manuscript competition for a first book of poetry.

When to my surprise I won, Betty helped me edit the manuscript. The harder I was on my work, cutting a line here, an entire poem there, the more she encouraged me. Betty regarded the ability to edit oneself as among the greatest attributes of a writer, and she believed it was a skill that could be learned. Looking back on the book, which I entitled *Falling Off* to capture my uneasiness in New York, my sense of the city as a place where one might indeed fall off the world and disappear, I am grateful for Betty's wisdom and discretion. She allowed me to be who I was—a slowly maturing twenty-four-year-old, still very much a poet in training—but she also saw to it that I made the very best book of which I was capable at the time.

Not long after the book was published, as we were toiling over one of the Academy's programs, Betty made an offhand remark that shocked me. She was a thorough professional when it came to the detail work, and while I tried to be conscientious, I had goofed something up, and was busy trying to set it right. I said I hoped she wasn't disappointed in me, and she paused a moment before replying. Catching my eye, she said, "No. I would be disappointed in you if you were still in this job ten years from now."

Chapter

Four

FALLING OFF

I SOMETIMES THINK EVERYTHING THAT HAPPENED to me as a young woman in New York City can be traced to a dress. I reported for work at the Guggenheim Museum in January 1969 in a state of great anticipation, wearing an olive-green shift, plain but for some ribbing in the fabric. I looked forward to hearing Bill Knott and Ron Loewinsohn read that night, and as I had been living in the 1960s college uniform of T-shirts and bell-bottom jeans, I felt that the occasion warranted a dress. Made of "bonded polyester," a rubbery new fabric which in hindsight seems more appropriate for industrial sponges than apparel, my dress had appealed to me because of its low price—I had picked it out of a discount bin at a small department store in Bennington—and its shapelessness. In my teens I had grown self-conscious of my body, and this dress provided ample covering.

That evening, my job consisted of following Betty around before and after the reading, learning the ropes. It wasn't until late at night, when we were preparing to leave the museum, that she asked me where I had gotten the dress. I told her. And she said, in a regal manner that was at once critical and kind, "It does not suit you. You have a nice figure, you could show it off. The long line is good on you, but you need something with more form. And a brighter color would be more flattering to your complexion." Betty's careful assessment was undeniably true, and left me feeling more chastened than angry. If my mother had said all this to me, I might have been resentful, and resistant to the common sense behind the words. My mother has always had a sense of style, and when I was a teenager she was mystified to have raised a daughter with so little regard for it.

Betty was then in her early fifties, not anyone's mother, and suddenly I could see myself as she saw me: a young woman hiding herself in clothes meant for a matron, a hideous dress whose drab color drained my already pale face. In a feeble attempt at self-defense, I said that it had cost me very little, as if thrift could justify the purchase of something so ugly. Betty sighed, and offered to take me shopping at her favorite resale shop on the East Side, just a few blocks from the Academy. I found myself assenting, reluctant but intrigued.

In the matter of clothing, as with so much else, Betty was adept at stirring me out of my schoolgirl complacency. Her eye for quality, simplicity, and style was such that I still wear a pair of shoes that she once insisted I buy, dismissing my objection that they were impractical and pricey. I am now the age Betty was when I met her, and much of the wisdom that she casually imparted still carries weight with me, as I observe women and fashion. Women who consistently wear modish clothing that is not right for their body type, she said, have inner conflicts that no amount of fashion will cure. She pointed out that as they age, women often keep the hairstyle and makeup they wore at the peak of their sexual desirability. She demonstrated this principle as we rode together on a New York City bus, opening my eyes to the fact that we were surrounded by women aging ungracefully in elaborate caked makeup and improbably colored hair, epitomes of chic from the thirties, forties, and fifties.

The North Carolina poet William Harmon was disarmed by Betty, when, after a reading honoring him as the recipient of the Academy's Lamont award, then given for a first book of poetry, she complimented him on the wit and energy of his reading style and on his natty attire. She then suggested that he consider changing his hairstyle. When the poet later asked me whether she treated everyone in this manner, I replied that Betty would go that far only with someone she liked. I asked him if he had decided she was right about the hair, and he said he was surprised to find he had. It worked that way more often than not, I told him, and he had gotten off easy; normally Betty would have supplied the name and address of a friendly barber.

Betty could be a formidable woman, but her attentions were not in the least oppressive, because they obviously came from a generous and hospitable impulse. The last thing she wanted was to make anyone over in her own image. She was like the gifted writing teacher who sets about to help her students find their own voice, and who would be horrified if any of them settled for imitating her. As a boss, Betty had a blessedly relaxed managerial style: as long as the work was done properly, and on time, we were free to play hooky.

She introduced me to her own neighborhood haunts, all within walking distance of the Academy: a pastry shop and tea room called Mrs. Herbst's; the Ideal, a greasy-spoon in Yorkville that served hearty German food; and sprawling charity thrift stores a few blocks east of the Academy on Third Avenue. On one memorable excursion, made when we were both feeling restless and let down after a reading and reception the night before, Betty found drapes for her Manhattan apartment, and I purchased three lined linen sheaths, an entire summer wardrobe, for the sum of $12.50. They evidently had been made by a dressmaker for a wealthy client, and fit me perfectly. They also converted my mother, who had been horrified that I was buying used clothing.

Betty would gently chide me about how I held to provincial ways, still considering, for example, certain clothes to be "Sunday best." She disliked my tendency to hoard new things, as if I had to save them against some future need. Once, when she sharply reminded me that clothing is meant to be used and that storage can ruin it, I knew she was speaking of more than fabric. Betty sensed that I was a basically fearful young person, afraid of my life, afraid of my vocation as a poet, afraid of love, and that this had led me to hoard my emotions along with my clothes.

New York was an improbable place for me; my shyness and trepidation put me at odds with Manhattan's brash atmosphere. Like many young writers Betty had known, I had been attracted to the city for its prodigious energies, so wonderful and terrible, only to find that I had to struggle against myself to survive there. The daimon of the city, like the genius of poetry itself, could be both nurturing and destructive. It seemed all wrong, yet I chose to come to terms with my life and art there.

Many years later, during Betty's last summer, she invited me to help her sort through her personal papers. Illness had sapped her energy, and I ended up taking many boxes home. Going through them at my leisure, I was enchanted by a description Betty had made, in middle age, of the young woman she had been when she arrived in Manhattan in the late 1940s. She could have been describing me, when, full of insecurity and its attendant bravado, I had dared to see if I might become a real New Yorker. In a few paragraphs, Betty had captured what I thought coming to the city would mean, and what I thought I'd left behind, and she also articulated the dire importance, in Manhattan, of appearances:

> *When I first came to New York, that immunity the city grants a newcomer covered me like a corn husk. I felt untouched, invulnerable, at a virginal distance. The city seemed a game I could enter or leave at will. . . . I had that grey suit. I wore it because it was my best. I could be a careless young woman in a suit that cost $125. And Susan [a relative] walked next to me, buoying me up. How dead she is—twenty years now. Mother had just died, and Susan bought me the suit as a consolation.*
>
> *I must have looked attractive. Sometimes the mirror said yes, but I needed more than that. I'd look for approval in people's faces. I was never sure. I wore the grey suit in Manhattan's terrible heat and looked for a job.*
>
> *All of my dead (some of them then living) were helping me enter New York; I see that now that I no longer have them. But then I thought they were hindrances, to be shoved aside, repressed, diminished. The incredible professionalism of New Yorkers hit me more than anything else, and it seemed to me then*

as now that I'd always be an amateur. I could never escape my
background.

I did not have a stylish outfit, but a bulky wool pantsuit that
my grandmother Norris had painstakingly sewn for me. My grandmother Totten, who could have provided me with expensive clothing from a department store, was much too frugal to do so. She did
mail me several pairs of gloves. Born in 1891 in rural Virginia, she
knew that no lady was properly attired for a city without a hat and
white gloves.

AFFAIRS

The gloves were pristine and out of place, an undecipherable message from a sane, well-ordered world to one that was confused and
messy. I was then flirting with disasters that my grandmothers could
barely imagine. After Betty Kray offered me the two-month job at
the Academy, the professor with whom I was infatuated, but who
was not yet my lover, offered to help me find a short-term rental. He
took me to visit Ultra Violet, a French heiress who was an Andy
Warhol superstar, and rumored to be the mistress of Salvador Dalí.
At the time she was looking for a boarder to rent a room in her large
apartment near the Guggenheim Museum. It would have been an
ideal location for me, as I would be able to walk to work. I had seen
photographs of Ultra Violet in the underground press, but she was
much more beautiful in person. She seemed amused by me and
flirted with my escort as if I were not there. I didn't mind; she was
fascinating to watch. But I could only wonder what those two

months would have been like, as it was clear she would not tolerate living with a younger woman, especially one as gauche as I.

I found a place through Bennington, a bed in a cramped Yorkville apartment that I shared with two friendly and slightly older women who had secretarial jobs and were looking for husbands. I listened incredulously to their tales of cruising for young men at Bloomingdale's and the singles bars that thrived on the Upper East Side. When I began my affair with the married professor, they assumed he had agreed to leave his wife, and were appalled when I revealed that this was the last thing I wanted. The affair made everything more intense, and added to the glamour that had first attracted me to New York. But I soon felt I had sneaked into the city under false pretenses, under the wing of my professor, who introduced me to writers, artists, art critics, and museum curators, all of whom seemed impressively urbane, and settled in comfortable, book-lined apartments or vast studios humming with creative energy. Seduced by an exhilarating convergence—the poetry I had studied with him in college, his wit and sophistication, the exciting New York scene of which he was a part—I imagined that I was living the life I was destined for. But it was his world I was drawn into, and I was there by his sufferance. His friends and colleagues often treated me callously, as if I were not fully human, but only his "girl," or more accurately, his "latest girl."

At a party, one of them, placing his hand on my knee with an insinuating assurance, suggested that once my lover was through with me, I might take up with him. "He'll never leave his wife, you know," he told me, and although it hurt to hear it stated so bluntly, I put on a poker face and said that I did know. Impressed by the gratuitous cruelty of his remark, I removed his hand from my thigh.

Had I not been ready to hear the truth, it might have been devastating. My situation was precarious, and my cowardly attempt to test the waters of love by getting involved with someone who was already committed had led me to dangerous seas. When, over the next year, as I matured and hungered for more intimacy, I did not know how to read the signs that my lover was already looking for another girl, one who would be less demanding and more pliable, someone younger and needier than I. Perhaps only a twenty-one-year-old could have been blindsided by this turn of events.

I had kept this relationship hidden from Betty, because I knew it would displease her, and the man was a friend of hers. But when he started to break it off, she could tell from my behavior that something was wrong. Without asking what the trouble was, she spirited me away for a weekend in the creaky two-hundred-year-old Rhode Island house she and her husband had purchased in the 1950s. Her excuse was that she wanted the company, as Vladimir was away. Set on a considerable acreage, with hayfields surrounded by a forest of evergreens, oaks, mulberry trees, and a variety of maples, the farm was a godsend. I could see the stars at night, and during the day I threw myself into chores. To help Betty prepare the soil for her vegetable garden, I collected compost in a wheelbarrow. As I shoveled, I was observed by a large black snake that followed my movements like a spectator at a tennis match and made me laugh. Later Betty and I drove to her favorite beach, Moonstone, and let the ocean waves massage us. We gathered thick strands of seaweed to take back for her compost pile.

As Betty prepared our supper, I spilled out the story. She took the news calmly, clearly wanting me to move on. "Your first love affair is over," she commented. "Put it behind you, and remember that if a man will cheat on his wife, he will cheat on you." She said that affairs with older poets had been the bane of young women who worked at the Academy, and that my situation was far less disastrous than some. Betty had faith in me, and was counting on my practicality and good sense, even if I had demonstrated a lack of both.

This gave me hope, and that night I was awakened by moonlight shining on my face. It was as if the full moon were offering me consolation, saying, *Maybe he did love you once, get some sleep.* And I slept. But the next morning I was full of dread over the seemingly insurmountable task of letting go. I could no longer presume to share in my lover's life, but in the new dispensation would have to build a life of my own. My turbulent desires mystified me: I longed to cling to the relationship and briefly harbored thoughts of becoming pregnant, as though that could help me preserve some of the initial joy that I had felt in the romance. I have since been told by battered women that pregnancy often suggests itself to them in this way, just when they are beginning to pull themselves out of an abusive situation, as though it could help them make something good come out of something so bad. I thank God that I knew that a child was the last thing I needed. Getting pregnant then would have been a self-destructive act, and I am not sure I would have survived.

Betty was a great help during this period when I was, predictably enough, spending my nights weeping to Billie Holiday and Janis Joplin. I took up smoking more pot than was good for me, simply because it relieved the pain. And I resolved never again to engage in the cruel, demeaning, exhausting subterfuges of adultery. The one time I slipped up, indulging in an amiable overnight liaison with an out-of-town poet, I was prepared to deal with the aftermath. When the man wrote me a frenzied letter in which he said he was leaving his wife and small child and moving to New York so that we could be together, I recognized the letter for what it was, a fiction

that had little to do with me. He might as well have been writing to
an imaginary love, or a muse. I responded immediately that while I
liked him very much, his place was with his family, and that if he
came to New York, I would not see him, or even speak to him. I
showed both letters to Betty, who said simply, "You did the right
thing." The man saw the sense of it as well, and remained a friend,
but from a distance.

MISERABLE MIRACLE

In the midst of this period in which I was starting to come into my
own, struggling to make a life for myself on the giddy New York poetry scene, the best and worst that could have happened did. I attained some success as a poet. Early in 1971, when the Chicago poet
Paul Carroll came to read for the Academy at the Guggenheim,
Betty introduced me as a young poet working in the office. Carroll
asked me what I was writing, and I told him about the angel handbook. He encouraged me to enter a first-book competition he had
founded at Big Table Books. I told him I didn't have a manuscript
ready yet. I was too depressed to attend the party after Carroll's
reading—I had encountered my former lover at the museum, and he
had been distant and dismissive. I feared that the party would bring
more of the same, and as I watched people fill taxicabs to go to the
party, I decided to go home. I forgot about Paul Carroll's request until he wrote to me, asking to see the angel poem and anything else I
could send. I mailed him the bundle of poems that Jane Cooper had
been trying to convince me was a book, and Carroll wrote back a few
months later to tell me that I had won the contest. I would have a
book published by Big Table that fall.

I was elated, but stunned, and soon learned that my success was a mixed blessing. The book was like an earthquake, shaking the fault lines of my life. Then as now, New York City was a mecca for artists looking for the breaks—gallery exhibitions, publications, stage roles—that help them become established. Betty liked to remind me that even Robert Bly, who by the late 1960s was back in his native Minnesota, had earlier paid his literary dues in New York. She spoke of him wearing an old top hat to readings, and of donning his college tie when he visited E. E. Cummings, so that the two men could "play Harvard," trying to outdo each other with literary anecdotes from their respective days on campus.

The atmosphere of literary Manhattan in the early 1970s could be stifling and incestuous, with the same people always attending the same readings and parties. It was also highly competitive. I was one of many hopefuls who arrived in the city each year fresh out of college, looking for jobs to support the writing habit. Within a few years, some would enroll in business or law school and stop writing entirely. Others would return to their hometowns, to write human-interest stories for the local newspaper and work on novels or books of poems. And a few hung on in the city, networking with editors, publishers, and literary patrons, keenly aware of the other young writers trying to build a name for themselves.

The Big Table prize made me one of the first of my generation to break out of the pack, and once it was announced, people who would otherwise have ignored me began to pay attention. Previous winners had been Bill Knott and Andrei Codrescu, who were well-regarded poets. But I was an unknown, with few publications except in the Bennington literary magazine. Word of the award cast a chill on my budding friendships with some student poets in the graduate writing programs that were then proliferating. For MFA candidates seeking college teaching positions, publish-or-perish was a harsh reality, and I sometimes felt resented as an interloper, with my book taking up a slot that should have gone to someone who needed it to get a job. I resorted to the defensive tactic of not talking about the book at all. William Harmon told me that when he came to read for the Academy in 1971, it took him some time to realize that the young woman camouflaged as a microphone tester was in fact a poet, and one with a book coming out. He had expected that any young writer would have been shouting such good news from the rooftops.

But I had grown wary, having been discouraged by the negative responses of acquaintances and people I considered friends. My roommate at the time, a Juilliard student, had become tense with a jealousy I could not comprehend, as she was herself a gifted musician and composer. Her evening practice on the small piano in our apartment—Bartók, Chopin, Bach, Mendelssohn—was one of the joys of my life, and I was hurt when she reported to our friends that all I wanted was to become famous. Now that I was to publish, her student status rankled, and the wedge that my success drove between us made our living situation a trial. She left the city not long after my book came out, and it was many years before we could restore our friendship.

As for my former teacher and lover, he had told Betty that I would never amount to anything without him, and saw my publication award as an affront. To have him out of my life was just as well, but it was not easy to hear from people who knew us both the bad things he was saying about me. It was a confusing time. While some old friends were jealous and resentful, others were newly attracted to me because of my success. I felt extremely isolated, and it was difficult to know whom to trust. At one party after a reading, I entered into a conversation with Gerard Malanga, the poet and photographer who had long been Andy Warhol's assistant. I had first become aware of Gerard at college, when other Bennington students reported breathlessly on his infamous dancing, with a bullwhip as a prop, in concerts by the prototypical punk band the Velvet Underground. When I met him, and we talked for a while, I discovered that I liked him.

Gerard tried to impress on me the significance of winning a publication prize and offered me advice on promoting the book. When I mentioned that my parents had lost their nerve when naming me for my aunt Kathleen Dakota Norris, choosing the milder "Kathleen Anne," Gerard suggested that I rechristen myself "Dakota Norris." His proposal was in the spirit of the times, the heyday of the Warhol superstars—models, debutantes, actors, and hangers-on who assumed new identities as International Velvet, Ondine, Viva, Ultra Violet, Ingrid Superstar, and Billy Name. And while I disregarded his advice, I decided Gerard was good company. After we left the party together, we sat and talked for hours on a bench in Riverside Park. I ended up going home with him.

That evening, with its elements of farce and grace, is one I will always treasure. If nothing else, it is a prime example of how things that start out all wrong can sometimes come out right. Half tipsy, Gerard and I did the expected thing, performing the great ritual of the "sexual revolution," toppling into bed with little thought of the consequences. Just after we had made love, as I was still savoring the simple comforts of body warmth, he turned to me and said, "Tell me, how long is your book going to be?" That was the last question I wanted to hear, and I thought of Honolulu all of a sudden, and how far away my family was. But Gerard was so pleasant and friendly that my despondency lifted. Later, he introduced me to his photographs of Cybill Shepherd, Lotte Lenya, Mick Jagger, Bob Dylan, and

William Burroughs, which remain some of the best portraits I have ever seen: in them the viewer sees first an ordinary human face, and only gradually recognizes a face seen many times before. As we talked I hoped I had found a friend, someone who, despite his rakish reputation, was sensible and kind.

Gerard was rich in ambiguities: a street-wise but essentially gentle person, soft-spoken with the trace of a Bronx accent, ambitious enough as an artist to be able to survive in New York, yet not terribly jealous of the success of others, particularly if he thought it well deserved. In those days he looked like an Adonis, but he didn't seem overly vain. "A prince and a punk" is how he once described a pet cat to me, and it was not a bad description of Gerard himself. He was a tough guy capable of writing a poem in memory of a lovely model in her early twenties who had killed herself, a woman he had photographed in Paris standing on a rooftop, looking not glamorous but merely young. I remember being haunted by her face in magazine shampoo advertisements after her death. In his poem Gerard speaks of his desire to bring her back to life, if only in his photographs: "Come to life in the dark room / of a developing tray / containing the water of silence / which is now your grave." He concludes his poem with a blessing: "A memory looking for a past to be present / exists in the photos / be happy, wherever you are."

His black leather outfits notwithstanding, Gerard could be maternal in his attentions, and he was one of the people who helped me survive my early twenties. By unspoken agreement, we decided early on that we were much better friends than lovers, and that is how it has remained between us, for some thirty years. In the early 1970s he showed he was the sort of friend who could be relied on for good advice. Taking psychedelic drugs was then regarded as hip and a test of character. The myth was that the truly cool, the bold and strong, would have good trips, while lesser mortals would become unhinged. I had, accordingly, felt ashamed when marijuana began to make me paranoid, and when my one and only experience of LSD terrified me so much that I spent much of the trip, nearly ten hours, curled in fetal position, sound asleep. But the worst experience had been with some mescaline that my roommate brought home one Friday afternoon, a gift from another Juilliard student. I should have known better than to take such a drug, given the tensions between us, and the disruptions of that year. But I took it anyway, and paid the price. I went to see Gerard soon after, in his illegal sublet a few blocks south of the Academy on Madison Avenue. I described my bad trip, and Gerard said, simply, "If you can't handle drugs, you have no business taking them." He had seen enough self-destruction in the Warhol crowd to know his limits, and reminded me that I had better know mine.

I might have thought twice about the mescaline had I been familiar with the writer and artist Henri Michaux's book about the drug, aptly titled *Miserable Miracle*, in which he describes mescaline as "the enemy of poetry, and meditation, and above all of mystery." The drug had made me feel as if I had been inhabited by an "it," a word-making machine that I could not turn off. I might stop speaking, but it ran on and on inside my head, like a ticker-tape dispenser of stock market quotes. Words themselves became oppressive, and suddenly my entire life seemed false and unendurable.

I was experiencing what Michaux describes as the "mescaline hurricane," in which a thought blows into one's mind and disintegrates, with another thought following closely, only to repeat the pattern. After a while, he writes, you become "wholly uninhabitable, horrifying to yourself, your house in the torrent, an object of ridicule in your own eyes." It's a hell of a way to spend a Friday night, Good Friday, as it happened. All my self-doubts rose up to mock me, and I wondered whether my life in New York was just a fantasy I was maintaining to avoid responsibility for much of anything. I dismissed my poems as mere anesthesia.

The legend of the vampire is that it can never go where it has not been invited, and by ingesting the drug, I had allowed a monster access to my inmost self. I was afraid to go to sleep that night, and sat instead at the card table that my roommate and I used for meals, holding on to it with both hands, convinced that if I let go, even once, I would throw myself from our rooftop terrace, more than twenty stories above the ground. I did not want to trouble my roommate; it didn't seem fair to wake her, and I did not know how to describe the torment I was in. Not until first light did I dare to get up to use the bathroom, and pour myself a glass of water.

Later that morning my roommate asked whether she should take me to a hospital, but I thought that if I rested awhile, I would be all right. Unaccustomed to her solicitude, I began to cry when she prepared half a grapefruit for me, and tried to explain that I had been thinking of the scene in a James Cagney movie in which he smashes a cut grapefruit into a woman's face. She was only feeding me, which made me inexpressibly grateful, but my words came out as nonsense. I slept for most of that day, and on Sunday was able to walk with her to the apartment of a musician friend who lived with a Rockette, a friendly woman named Barbara. She had cooked an Easter buffet, and the good food, combined with her warm hospitality, did much to ease my mind. But the grip of mescaline made preparing for work on Monday morning a terror. I looked at my shoes on the closet floor and was afraid to put them on. Somehow I managed. Henri Michaux says that mescaline effects an "experimental schizophrenia," and it does wear off. Still, it took weeks before I could ride the subway without suffering an offhand temptation to throw myself on the tracks.

CAREER

Betty was in Salt Lake City when I ingested the drug. Her husband, who was now emeritus in the music department at Columbia, had accepted an invitation to spend part of each year teaching at the University of Utah, and Betty was glad for the opportunity to join him occasionally in the West. Her frequent letters and postcards were like jolts of sanity, full of impressions of the Great Salt Lake, the dramatic vistas of Zion National Park, and Indian petroglyphs in a cave she had visited. Her experience of the petroglyphs inspired a poem by her good friend Adrienne Rich, "Burning Oneself Out":

> *You told me of setting your hand*
> *into the print of a long-dead Indian*
> *and for a moment, I knew that hand,*

> *that print, that rock,*
> *that sun producing powerful dreams*

Betty was quick to respond to the letter I sent her relating my experience of mescaline. "I think I need to live better," I had written, trying to convey my lingering unease. Even the fact that I couldn't decide on a title for my poetry manuscript took on a new significance. Paul Carroll favored "Excerpts from the Angel Handbook," but I resisted, although I was struggling to come up with an alternative. "I see the poems as evasions," I told Betty, "desiring to present an ordered self, as I want to be." The edgy reaction of so many friends and acquaintances to news of my award had caused a deeper unrest in me than I could acknowledge at the time. Why, I asked myself, did I need to publish a book in the first place?

It had been easy to write poetry at Bennington, which had a well-deserved reputation for nurturing young artists, actors, dancers, and writers. But as Louise Bogan, a practical woman who had supported herself and her child by writing book reviews, once remarked, it was also "a three-times removed from reality kind of place." No small part of the unreality for me was that poetry mattered there. But after I graduated, I soon discovered that the world would not care if I never wrote another poem. I had come to the city not knowing what I wanted, and was content to put off decisions about my future, assuming that I would enjoy the job at the Academy until I got serious about making a living. Then I would return to school and pursue a career. I did not think of poetry in terms of a "career." At Bennington I had placed a few poems in literary periodicals—the first in *Tennessee Poetry Journal*—and while publication boosted my ego and spurred new ambitions for my work, I had little idea what these ambitions would entail.

New York granted me the opportunity to see pure ambition in action. When I met the poet Patti Smith at a party given by Gerard Malanga, she seemed possessed by a desire for fame so strong that even dressed like a scarecrow in the midst of a group of gaudy transvestites, self-proclaimed "Chelsea Girls," she commanded attention. Smith described how her idol, Bob Dylan, had happened into the bookstore where she worked, and how, after selling him some books, she had gone out to the street and sat on the curb, sobbing. The encounter convinced her that she had to quit her job and devote her energies to writing. Later in the evening, when I stepped onto the fire escape for a breath of fresh air, I found Smith examining an abandoned robin's egg. We stood there awhile, talking quietly and listening to the sounds of the city at night. Her energy and nerve impressed me, and I felt that her decision to write full-time was noble, if foolhardy. In February 1971, at a reading she and Gerard Malanga gave at St. Mark's-in-the-Bowery, an event now routinely described as a turning point in the history of rock and roll, I learned that Smith had developed a unique style, rock poetry half sung, half chanted to the accompaniment of an electric bass. She left her audience exhilarated, and I rode the subway home believing more than ever in the power of art to illuminate and transcend the ordinary.

Even in the tamer environs of the poetry world, one could find people driven by ambition, poets setting their caps for sizable grants that would allow them to write in Europe for a year, publication with a prestigious publisher, or a prize teaching position. The phrase "careerist poet" seems a contradiction in terms, a quaint concept in these days of dot-com millionaires. But in the early 1970s, a time of great ferment in all the arts in America, a new generation of poets was bent on making itself known. Erica Jong, for example, when she was still a graduate student at Columbia, often said she was determined to produce a bestseller that would make her a household name. She wrote *Fear of Flying* with that in mind, and it worked.

Although the Academy offered several plums—a good reading series and well-regarded poetry awards—I rarely got hustled, as most people knew that my position involved more typing than powerbrokering. One poet did pursue me, suggesting with a portentous air when we happened to meet at readings that "we must get together." One day she called to set a date for lunch at an expensive restaurant; lamentably, in all my time at the Academy, it was the only such invitation I received. In an uneasy moment over our meal, I told her that my opinions carried no weight whatsoever with the judges for the Lamont competition, and that at any rate her book, having already been published, was not eligible. She then wanted only to be rid of me as soon as possible, and rushed me through the rest of lunch so mercilessly that I was reminded of the Buster Keaton comedy in which he finds that he must eat faster and faster in order to get any food at a boardinghouse table. Now that I was of no use to her, the poet dropped me entirely, and took to deluging a bemused Betty Kray with invitations to dinner parties.

As I watched this poet and others build their reputations step by painstaking step, I realized I did not have the energy to follow suit. I was still having difficulty coping with even the small amount of success I had attained. For years I had enjoyed being an anonymous, invisible person, one who listens and observes from the corner of the room. I had managed to create safe havens for myself at Bennington and in New York City, making of these unlikely places cloisters in which I could daydream and write in peace. Most of my weekends in Manhattan I spent in solitary pursuits, revising and typing poems in the Academy office in the mornings, and then walking, browsing in bookstores, and attending foreign films. But in the early 1970s, my YMHA "Discovery" reading, followed by the Big Table publication prize, forced me into a public identity as a poet before I was able to cope with it.

It was a difficult time to come to terms with this aspect of a literary life. What I witnessed in New York was a precursor to America's celebrity culture of the 1990s. It was during this period that the word *superstar* came into the lexicon, at first in an ironic sense, used by the actors in Andy Warhol's underground films, who were famous only in Manhattan. But the underlying notion took hold, for good or ill, that people are either "somebody" or "nobody," the latter rendered invisible by the light of the stars nearby. Whatever the field of endeavor, from poetry to medicine, there are always so many somebodies in New York that the pressure to succeed is relentless. The danger is that in constantly measuring one's work against that of others, one may lose sight of what it means to be true to oneself.

In this charged and seductive environment, I couldn't have asked for a better mentor than Betty Kray, who once said, after looking over a slick promotional brochure that a poet had mailed her, "What is a poet's career, but the writing of poems?" Betty kept me focused on the poems themselves, and on continuing to develop my art. She was willing to accept both me and my work as we were at the time: promising, but still in formation, in need of nurturing rather than promotion. Betty pushed me only as an honest and perceptive reader—if, in reading a poem, she said, "I begin to lose you here," I would know she had found a weak spot, lines that needed work. She left me on my own to pursue publication and other forms of recognition as a poet. It would not have occurred to her to try to use her influence to help me win an award or a grant, or place a poem in a magazine. And I wouldn't have asked. Whenever a poet requested that Betty endorse an application for a grant such as the Guggenheim, she would demur, saying that it was much better to obtain recommendations from peers. Whatever power Betty had she used for poetry itself, because she believed in the art.

PILGRIM'S PROGRESS

One would hardly think that the publication of a small book of verse could be so disruptive, but *Falling Off* turned my life inside out, and made such wreckage of the year 1971 that it seemed a good idea to retreat at Christmas. I offered to tend a friend's apartment while he visited his parents for the holidays. Gerard Malanga was between apartments then, and late on Christmas Eve, when he phoned and discovered that I was alone, he invited me to the place where he was house-sitting. I took a brisk walk down Broadway near midnight on the clear, starry night, some twenty blocks with no company except a few harmless drunks. I found Gerard comfortably installed in an architect-designed townhouse, the home of a comic-book heiress, complete with furniture in chrome and leather, and a glossy mink coverlet on a king-size bed. There was very little food in the house, but we thawed some frozen won ton soup for a meal. In the morning we took a long walk through a magically snowy Central Park. Gerard could not afford much film in those days, yet he used an entire roll on me, sitting in front of the Bethesda Fountain or posing on a granite outcropping by the lake. To warm up afterward we walked to a Jewish delicatessen on West Seventy-ninth Street and shared a plate of blintzes. It was one of the best Christmases of my life.

Back in my solitude at my friend's apartment, I had time to reflect on the mess I had made of the previous year, when I had reacted to feeling unloved by acting unlovable. I was relieved to find so many friends still there when the smoke cleared, people like Betty, Gerard, and Jean Valentine, who were genuinely glad for my success and had been willing to wait for me to grow up when I didn't handle it very well.

I was not prepared, however, for what the book had done to my writing. Once it was published, an internal fog set in, and I did not write anything presentable for another three years. I learned the hard way that poets can experience publication as a kind of death. And for poets who publish when they are still very young, as I did, this process can be especially painful. I had been diffident about my writing all along, and once I had a book, I had little faith that I could ever write another. A small grant that I received from the New York State Council on the Arts only deepened my sense of dislocation. When an older poet tried to talk me into applying for a Guggenheim grant—he either was on the board or had some pull with those who were—I backed off, telling him that I was not ready. Betty agreed with my assessment.

The poet James Tate was a great help to me during this period. His own first book, *The Lost Pilot*, had won a prestigious Yale Younger Poets award when he was twenty-one, and he told me that his writing had dried up for a long time afterward. My book hadn't enjoyed (or deserved) the acclaim in the poetry world that his had received, although it did elicit favorable reviews in *Library Journal* and *The Village Voice*. I told Tate I didn't mind that my book had settled on bookstore shelves, where most copies remained unsold. He understood my postpartum depression, and gave me good, brotherly advice. Tate was a kindred spirit in many ways. He was also an outsider, a midwesterner in the East, and while I never got to know him well, when we did get together I sensed we were the Bobbsey Twins gone bad, deranged in Manhattan, lost but able to laugh about it. We posed together in a twenty-five-cent photo booth, and toured a pornographic bookstore near Times Square, making fun of the images on the magazine covers. I recall him phoning once from La Guardia Airport, in near-ecstasy: he was sitting at a boarding gate with Little Richard and his entourage, and he just had to tell someone.

Betty Kray, with her vast experience of poets, understood the slump I was in, and nudged me out of it by foisting all manner of books on me—George Gissing's *The Odd Women*, Jean Toomer's *Cane*, Amos Tutuola's *The Palm-Wine Drinkard*, and *Wide Sargasso Sea* by Jean Rhys, whose vivid account of the first Mrs. Rochester sent me back to *Jane Eyre*. Betty continued to take me up to her place in Rhode Island on weekends, where the quiet beauty of the setting and the physical chores I performed were a much-needed restorative. On other weekends I might take the Long Island Rail Road to the end of the line at Montauk and rent a room in the off-season, spending my days walking the beach in the brisk winds and my nights trying to write. But even though I was diligently performing my duties at the Academy, I remained listless at heart. Betty suggested that I audit a class on the eighteenth-century novel that James Wright was teaching at Hunter College. "It will get you into conversations about books again," she said, "and open you up to other perspectives." Several days a week I took the subway to Hunter after work.

Wright's manner of teaching was a joy. Literature was not just a subject to him, but life itself. His voice thundering, he would say things that made all the difference in my ability to appreciate an otherwise remote book. About *The Pilgrim's Progress*, for instance, he said that the allegories were obvious, and not worth much elaboration. "They fall into place, and you can keep them at the back of your mind. What is important about this book, is that it was written by a man in prison." Under Wright's low-key but expert tutelage, eighteenth-century books came alive for me, not only Henry Fielding's *Tom Jones* but also Samuel Richardson's staid *Clarissa*. John Bunyan's *The Pilgrim's Progress* was my favorite by far, perhaps because it forced me to open a Bible, a book that had been important to me when I was younger but which I had neglected at college and in New York.

One night after class I met Gerard at Max's Kansas City, a bar and restaurant that was then the center of the universe for Manhattan's demimonde. It was an amazing place, always full of artists, actors, writers, poseurs, and crazies with their neuroses, and sometimes psychoses, worn in spangles on their sleeves. The fashionable back room was jammed with tables and chairs, and Warhol's set was present on most nights. One might be asked by Alice Cooper or Keith Richards to please pass the salt shaker.

I still think of Max's fondly, as a state-of-the-art den of iniquity that could be oddly beneficent in spirit. A Max's habitué, the transvestite actor Holly Woodlawn, described it in a memoir, *A Low Life in High Heels:* "The bacchanalian madness aside, Max's was perhaps the greatest group therapy I've ever known." Max's provided an alternative world where time stood still, the night never ended, and one could forget to go home. In Woodlawn's words, "It was as if I walked into the place when I was twenty-three and didn't walk out until I was twenty-five."

Still enthused from Wright's class, I carried my copy of *The Pilgrim's Progress* into Max's back room, and read passages aloud to Gerard. I loved the names: Great-Heart, Madame Bubble. And my favorite, Feeble-Mind, who never thinks he has the fortitude to complete his pilgrimage, but keeps going nonetheless. Finally, on the shores of the River Jordan, having willed his mind to a dunghill, he calls out to his friends, "Hold out, Faith and Patience!" as he crosses over. And the secret of Doubting Castle, where the pilgrim Christian and his companion Hopeful are held prisoner by the Giant Despair and his cruel wife, Diffidence, had great resonance for me. Just as it looks as if they will never escape, Christian says, "What a fool . . . am I, thus to lie in a stinking dungeon, when I might walk at liberty." He has remembered that he holds a key, called Promise, that would open any door in the castle. He has possessed this key all along, and had only to realize it—

I was interrupted by a beautiful young man who leaned across our table and asked if we were on a "heavy date." Gerard and I laughed, and said that we were talking about a book. "How dreadful!" he exclaimed, sidling into an empty chair. Gerard introduced him as a friend, Eric Emerson, who had acted in some of Andy Warhol's movies. He was stunning to look at, catlike in his movements, and told us wild stories, true or not, about traveling with the Rolling Stones, who kept both limos and drugs on call. Suddenly he took my hand. And looking intently into my eyes, he said, "I like your face. Would you have my baby?" My instinct was to laugh, but I was sober enough to realize that he wasn't joking. For all of his flamboyance, this was a fragile person I was addressing. "I don't think I can have anyone's baby," I said. "Oh, but I have such pretty ones," he replied, "all over the world, little blond babies. But I like your eyes. I want you to have my baby."

My God, I thought, I have met Narcissus. In the flesh. And Eric Emerson was a perfect Narcissus, to the end. Within a few years he would fall into what these days might pass for the pool of Narcissus, the dark depths of a drug overdose. And the others at the party where he died, his drug-addled friends, would take his corpse down to the street and leave it with his bicycle, trying to pretend that it had been a hit-and-run accident. I did not know this then, of course, and could not have foreseen it. But I knew that it was time to go home. I got into a cab in front of Max's, and turned down the driver's offer to share a joint. It was early in the morning and very cold. Dawn was not far off. From the West Side Highway, the skyline of my beloved Manhattan looked like a river of stars.

Chapter
Five

SALVATION
BY POETRY

Y LIFE HAD BECOME BIFURCATED. PART OF
me still wanted to be the good kid I had been brought up to
be, the Sunday-school girl formed in the Protestant work ethic. But
I had grown attracted to what was forbidden, all the things the good
girl had been denied.

In the fall of 1970, when the brutal "Mr. Goodbar" murder
took place only blocks from my apartment on the Upper West Side,
it hit uncomfortably close to home. The twenty-two-year-old victim
had been living the Catholic version of the virgin/whore dichotomy,
a modest parochial school teacher by day, a frequenter of singles bars
at night. The young man who had killed her explained to police that
he had grown angry when she asked him to leave after sex, telling
him she didn't want him around in the morning. I hoped I was safe

from that sort of violence; I did not go to singles bars and never picked up strangers. But I had become increasingly reckless with my life, and perhaps was closer to a bad end than I liked to think.

By the end of 1971, I had to face the fact that a rowdy nightlife was not conducive to writing or to maintaining my responsibilities at work. I might leave Max's at closing time, four A.M., and join a pack of people going to an artist's loft for a "rent party" in the newly residential SoHo. The loft's occupants would collect a few dollars from each person at the door to help pay the next month's rent. These parties were loud, with dancing to taped music and the strong scent of Colombian marijuana in the air. From there, I would either go home or sleep at a friend's apartment. After forcing myself awake at eight-thirty, I would take the subway to the office and sleep with my head on my desk until Dorothy arrived an hour later. Trying to live in both worlds, that of the day job I loved, and the dusk-to-dawn life I now craved, I was simply no match for those who, as Holly Woodlawn relates in her memoir, often slept until noon, had a breakfast of coffee, melba toast, and Methedrine, and spent the afternoon primping for the night to come.

One evening I encountered Woodlawn and Jackie Curtis, another well-known transvestite in the Warhol crowd, at a party for Lita Hornick's Kulchur Press, held at the Hornicks' elegant Park Avenue apartment. Together with a character named Rita Redd, they regaled me with hilarious stories. People who are high on speed can be very entertaining, and when I left the party with them, Rita was talking nonstop, being so outrageously funny that our cabdriver wiped tears of laughter from his eyes as he deposited us on a seedy block in Hell's Kitchen. We had arrived at Sanctuary, a former church that was now run as a "juice bar," an after-hours mostly gay dance hall where no alcohol was sold, but where you could buy any drug, and engage in all manner of sexual acts in the bathrooms or the former choir loft.

Still laughing, we paid our admission fees to men at the front door, whose suits bulged with shoulder holsters. The whiff of danger gave me pause, but not for long. With the others, I climbed the stairs to what was once the church sanctuary, where a raucous drag show was in progress. Later, people danced on the floor where pews had been, under the uncomprehending gaze of stained-glass windows. Manhattan's gay bars were, in the early 1970s, great places to dance, precursors of the disco craze. Sanctuary was featured in the movie *Klute* as the nightclub where the prostitute played by Jane Fonda goes to meet a powerful pimp and drug dealer. The menacing ambience was right on, but Hollywood had cleaned the place up considerably.

For some reason, that night, in that improbable environment, I began to get serious about my life. One of the gay men I met there, a quiet young hairstylist and aspiring actor who, like me, had decided to sit and watch the dancers, must have recognized that I was out of my element, and he asked me why I was at the club. I said that I had happened to come with a group of people after a party. But his probing made me feel that I was in a place where I did not belong, and if I persisted in hanging around, night after night, here or at Max's, I would be little more than a voyeur. I also had to acknowledge, over a memorable three days in which I had gotten all of seven hours' sleep, that I could not keep up the pace unless I started taking speed. And I am constitutionally unable to handle speed in any form. In college, on the rare occasions when I had to pull an all-nighter, a strong cup of coffee would usually suffice. If I needed something stronger, I could always ask friends for Dexedrine, but then I would appall them by taking a razor to the pill. Ingesting anything more than a third of a tablet in a night would be counter-productive, making me so edgy that I'd be unable to work at all. A knowing friend had told me that the mescaline I had recently taken was most likely cut with speed, and that was why it had devastated me.

As I observed the scene at Sanctuary, I realized that I was on the edge of an important decision. Uneasy and somewhat depressed, I entered the women's bathroom, where a young transvestite was reapplying makeup after what she told me had been a good cry. I replied that I could use a cry myself, and we talked for a while. It was about nothing I can remember now, only two strangers coming together for a moment of mutual consolation. She kindly offered me some makeup tips, for which I thanked her. Then I left and took a cab home.

I never returned to Sanctuary, but I have always been grateful for the night I spent there, among other young people who, like me, were struggling with questions of identity, of acceptance and rejection. Some, like Jackie Curtis, were eventually lost to drugs, others to the plague of AIDS. Some have survived. When I think of them I summon the comment of the early Church theologian Philo of Alexandria, who advised human beings to always "be kind, for everyone you meet is fighting a great battle."

Not long after that night, as I was sitting alone in my apartment on a sunny Saturday afternoon, the idea of goodness came, unbidden, into my mind, raising a question I had not thought of in a long time: What is sin? I described this moment in my book *Dakota:* "I thought I should know, but my mind was blank. I felt like the little boy in 'The Snow Queen,' who, as he is being carried off in the Queen's carriage, tries desperately to remember the Lord's Prayer but can think of nothing but the multiplication tables." I did suddenly remember my grandmother Totten, whose house in South Dakota I was to move into three years later, although I could not have imagined this at the time. But on that afternoon my grandmother's presence struck me with a poignancy that made me feel as if she were whispering in my ear over a distance of thousands of miles. And I wondered whether I did have a conscience, after all. It had come to seem a useless appendage, but now I suspected that it had simply been dormant. I was a Sleeping Beauty, awakened not by the kiss of a prince but by the resonant voice of my Presbyterian grandma.

A LIVING ART

After my book was published, I lost my voice to bouts of laryngitis that doctors diagnosed as psychosomatic. And while I worked at poems, they seemed dead on the page. Their words were never more than private scribbles, so tightly wound that I could not unravel them. In my writing as in my life, I was a girl adrift.

Ultimately, it was poetry that anchored me. At Betty's urging, I pored over documents in the Academy files, more than two hundred reports made by poets whom Betty had sent into junior high and high school classrooms in 1966. In her introduction to a 1967 *Urban Review* article that published a selection of these reports, Betty wrote: "We wanted the [students] to hear poetry, and to find out that poetry is to be listened to and enjoyed." It was her belief that poets, as practitioners involved more with the process of writing than with what she termed "the museum tour of poetry specimens" in textbooks and the typical English class, were uniquely suited to convey to both students and teachers "the pleasure to be found in knowing a living art."

I was interested to see that Betty and an ally at the New York City Board of Education had made certain that vocational schools were included along with schools preparing students for college. Betty believed that poetry belonged to everyone. And what I found in the reports of the poets, many not much older than I, changed the way I looked at the vocation of writing. Suffused with an optimism about the value of poetry to the human community that feels almost quaint today, the accounts made for lively reading.

Harvey Shapiro observed that while the students at first greeted him with "a kind of controlled hostility," they were also unguarded enough to listen and respond openly to the poems he read. And, he commented, "when these kids respond, there is no mistaking it. The language surprises them. They obviously don't expect to be moved by language, and they find it unsettling but pleasant—as if they've discovered a new kind of kick." After class, several students took time from their lunch hour to continue talking with him. Shapiro's approach, like that of most of the poets, was to talk not strictly about poetry, "but rather about why I write poetry"; once in the classroom, he determined that poetry was something the students had "already developed complete immunity to in school."

Among students in a Brooklyn school, Paul Blackburn reported, contemporary poems were "very useful in countering the general impression that poetry is part of the system summoned against them, something to be learned and hated." Furthermore, he wrote, "these kids have no literary sophistication, no education or pretense, and are really terrific." He found enthusiastic listeners, especially among teenage boys, for his translation of battle scenes from *El Cid*. And the students bombarded him with questions: "Do you write poems when they happen, right there, or wait until you get home? Why do you stop after every line?" This led Blackburn into a discussion of poetic prosody, and of how to listen to poetry, and to jazz.

As happened to most of the poets, Jay Wright's students pressed him to explain why they should bother with poetry. "The questions I received," he said, "were concerned with the relevance of poetry to life." In presenting a dazzling variety of material— Petrarch, Shakespeare, Yeats, Nicolás Guillén (in both Spanish and English), Langston Hughes, James Weldon Johnson, Wallace Stevens, Marianne Moore, LeRoi Jones (Amiri Baraka), and his own work—he learned that the students, while "they like simplicity and directness, will listen to anything if they think you believe in it and like it. Their openness to poetry is what I remember most."

Emmett Jarrett noted that teenagers were interested in the question of authenticity. "They wanted to know by what right I called myself a poet. Did I just write a few poems and say I was a poet, or did somebody big tell me I was? They also wanted to know how much money I made last year." He told them, only to find that they then wanted to discuss why anyone would become a poet "when there's no money in it." Still, he said, "they were not nearly as interested in that as they were in pursuing the thought in a given poem."

Ishmael Reed wrote that "the trick is to show them how the poetry they may or may not have read can be compared with the poetry they hear over the air waves." He used song sheets by Bob Dylan and other artists familiar to the students. Reed presented some of his own work and poems by his contemporaries Ed Field and Diane Wakoski. Initially the black students seemed self-conscious, and "a little nervous when I turned to the poems of the great Paul

Laurence Dunbar. But [they] 'hooped & hollared' when the rich-fun beauty-humour of this man's work came across."

My favorite reports, which I returned to whenever I had a spare moment in the office, were by Kathleen Fraser. In March 1966 she had appeared at a vocational high school whose students, nearly all girls, were training to be cosmeticians or dress-pattern cutters, and she read them poems about her own experiences as a child and teenager. "I tried to tell a little of the background of the poem," she wrote, "what I was like at the time, what I was feeling secretly, etc. I could feel the atmosphere in the room change quickly." The students, who had been described by teachers as "deficient in literary training," listened intently. Fraser's main concern, she said, "was to make them understand that poets were human beings who felt many things in common with [them] . . . and that poets simply tried to put these deep feelings into words." She also read them several poems that had attracted her as a teenager, García Lorca's "Song of the Seven-Hearted Boy" and Cummings's "in Just-Spring."

The girls were free with their questions to Fraser, and they asked her for recommendations of what poets they should read. "I think they would have liked to ask me where I bought my shoes," she wrote, "but they controlled themselves. But oh boy, were they checking out my clothes." She sensed that she had hit a nerve, by giving them the idea that poetry could speak to their hidden "yearning side." As she was leaving the school, two girls came up to her, and one asked, "Would you say you're a rebel?" When Fraser said yes, the girl turned to her friend, and said, "See. I told you!"

Even as I enjoyed Fraser's good humor, I was moved by her compassion for the students. She visited many schools in the city, some in impoverished neighborhoods. In one high school—which was "poorly equipped [but] with teachers who have lots of spunk"—a boy responded to her presentation by saying, "It sounds like your poetry is a very good friend you can tell everything to." At a junior high in a distressing slum, she encountered twelve- and thirteen-year-olds who seemed "fearful of their own ideas and feelings," languishing in the hands of a teacher who was obsequious with Fraser but "made her students feel degraded." Fraser wrote, "I felt so demoralized by the atmosphere in the room and the teacher's treatment of the kids (as she turned to me smiling and preening) that I wanted to reach out to them and let them know [that] they counted for something and that the way they saw things and felt things counted. I talked about city imagery, about the things I'd seen on their block, walking from the subway to their school, and tried to encourage them to look at things in new ways. They really didn't know what to think. But they were very sweet afterwards and had me autograph their hands."

A POETIC EDUCATION

These reports filled me with a new sense of what was possible with poetry. Clearly, it was much more than the exploration of one's feelings, or in the treasured phrase of adolescence, a form of "self-expression." Poetry was a discipline grounded in experience that drew its life and worth from a source much greater than oneself, and as it realized its potential to touch others in their innermost being, what Fraser had termed their "yearning side," it could be a profoundly communal act. Poetry, when it succeeded, did so in ways that were not quantifiable, and did not look much like worldly success, but that might be summed up as the joy on the face of a girl in a dingy classroom who finds a kindred spirit in a poem by García Lorca.

The reports in the Academy files chastised me, and forced me to acknowledge that I had become far too preoccupied with the trappings of literary success. In the hamlet that constitutes literary New York, I was tempted by careerism. But now poetry seemed a huge responsibility, one I was not sure I was ready to take on. How might I talk about writing to high school students, if I was asked? I doubted that anything I had written would be of interest to them, and had to ask myself why.

Kathleen Fraser had addressed each of those students as one human being to another, offering herself as a listener and a friend. If this is what poets do, I thought, then I had not much to offer. At the ripe age of twenty-four, having published one book of poetry, I felt spent, used up. But poetry, unlike mathematics, is not for prodigies. I might have been better off not publishing a volume of verse until my thirties or forties, but I did have Betty's faith in poets and poetry to challenge and invigorate me, and let me see how much I had yet to learn, and how little "success" had to do with it.

AN OUTCROPPING OF POETRY

In 1959, in a grant proposal to the Rockefeller Foundation, Betty had written that "it is clear that we are witnessing a new outcropping of American poetry, and it is rising from every corner of the continent." By the mid-1960s she was determined to send poets into classrooms to "reawaken in students the instinctual pleasure in language that very young children express so freely, but that goes dead later." Teachers were to be offered an in-service course conducted by older poets, and with an initial pledge of $10,000 from the Rockefeller Foundation (due, Betty said, to the imaginative support of Gerald Freund, who went on to become a legend at other philanthropic agencies, including the MacArthur Foundation), she was able to offer these programs to the New York City Board of Education free of charge. But she soon found that her plan was met with suspicion.

As she later recounted: "I was naive enough to think that [the Board] would welcome the offer." Instead, her proposed course for teachers, with a series of talks by poets—W. H. Auden on language, Anthony Hecht on imagery, Denise Levertov on sentiment and sentimentality, Robert Lowell discussing "what makes poetry modern," William Meredith and Robert Penn Warren on formal verse, Howard Nemerov on "how to read a poem," Louis Simpson on meaning in verse, W. D. Snodgrass on "the teacher and the poem"— was "flatly rejected by the in-service bureaucracy." Beyond the reason given, that these poets, many of whom were college professors, did not have the credentials to teach in the New York City schools, Betty sensed "a reflexive bureaucratic resistance to any idea extrinsic to departmental thinking." She wrote Freund that "we found ourselves explaining that we were not trying to teach a course on how to scan or to differentiate rhyme schemes; in fact, we found ourselves explaining that these poets are articulate." Once she got the courses going, however, they proved popular with teachers.

In 1967, the second year of these courses, Betty asked younger poets to address the teachers, among them Michael Benedikt, Louise Glück, Philip Levine, Ifeanyi Menkiti, Clarence Major, Adrienne Rich, and Theodore Weiss. One teacher enrolled in the class, William DeVoti, who moved to Connecticut in 1969 and enlisted Betty's aid in establishing a circuit for visiting poets among nine high schools there, described the course as "about the most exciting thing . . . in my academic career, meeting and talking with forty or so contemporary poets. . . . Nothing in college or graduate school came close to this."

Betty was energized by the responses of teachers such as De-Voti, who affirmed her sense that poets could share their hard-won understanding of how the words of ordinary language are transformed into a work of art. Artists, Louis Simpson has written, "have a body of knowledge that no one else has: a first-hand knowledge of process, the way a thing is made." The difference between the writer and the teacher, he says, is "the writer's knowledge of process, his ability to make the student understand a work from the inside out—as an organism rather than an object."

But poetry does not rest easily in the school curriculum, where it is chained to the study of grammar and even handwriting practice. It is still common, in elementary schools, to find the worst lines of Longfellow used to teach cursive writing. The students who make the neatest copies of the poem are rewarded by having their work placed in school hallways. The others, not unreasonably, conclude that poetry is irrelevant. Poetry is an art that can never be fully contained in the classroom, for, in William Stafford's words, the poem "will always be a wild animal. . . . There is something about it that won't yield to ordinary learning. When a poem catches you, it overwhelms, it surprises, it shakes you up. And often you can't provide any usual explanation for its power."

My own education in poetry followed an ordinary track. I had loved it as a small child, taking pleasure in reciting nursery rhymes and the like. But by eighth grade I had decided that poetry was beyond me, and I grew frustrated at trying to decipher the "hidden meanings" that my teachers said would become clear after repeated readings. Poetry didn't seem worth the effort. It wasn't wild at all, just a stupid intellectual game that poets played at the expense of schoolchildren.

It took an experienced practitioner of the art, Ben Belitt, to start me on the road to conversion. As my first literature professor at Bennington, he began to dismantle much of what I had learned about poetry in the previous twelve years. And after he encouraged me to write it myself, he guided me through my initial confrontation with the essential problem of poetry, that of finding the right words, those that offer the reader an experience that can't be stated in any other way. As Donald Hall has noted, in *Poetry: The Unsayable Said,* "The unsayable builds a secret room, in the best poems. . . . This room is not a Hidden Meaning, to be paraphrased by the intellect: it conceals itself from reasonable explanation. The secret room is something to acknowledge, to accept, and honor in a silence of assent: the secret room is where the unsayable gathers, and it is poetry's uniqueness."

Even after I had published a book of poems, I had yet to learn that the special power of a poem is its own, and does not make me special. I was lucky that my job at the Academy allowed me a good view of poets—not the majority, but a sizable number—who had become monsters of ego. And I could see that one might sacrifice one's humanity for nothing, having very little talent for poetry to begin with. One man became for me the ultimate cautionary tale. A self-published poet who regularly sent the Academy letters demanding that he be included in the reading series, he was consumed with rage at a host of literary institutions that failed to appreciate his genius. A friend of his reported that most evenings after work, he would settle in an easy chair, get drunk, and play at top volume tapes of himself reading his poems. Many nights he fell asleep to the sound of his own voice. A more self-contained, self-perpetuating prison I could not imagine, and recalling Dante, I envisioned the man as willfully having taken up residence in one of the lesser circles of hell.

THE NEW POETS

In 1957, the year Betty received her first grant to support readings by young poets at the 92nd Street Y, a breakthrough anthology appeared, *The New Poets of England and America*, edited by Donald Hall, Robert Pack, and Louis Simpson, who were themselves part of a new and prolific postwar generation of poets. Betty said of the period that "one knew that all over the country poets were writing, but the impact of the quantity, of the divergences, hadn't yet hit." An editor told her that in 1955, when he began working on the anthology, he had not known most of the poets included. When another anthology, Donald Allen's *The New American Poetry*, appeared in 1960, this editor found it remarkable that the book had no poets in common with the earlier collection.

The new poets were not always warmly received by established poetry institutions, which had grown to depend on well-known writers such as Robert Graves and Carl Sandburg to draw large audiences. At the YMHA Poetry Center, Robert Frost appeared every year from 1955 to 1961, and John Malcolm Brinnin, E. E. Cummings, Archibald MacLeish, Marianne Moore, and Stephen Spender appeared almost as often. Although the capacity audiences provided necessary financial support for the readings, Betty feared that the series was wearing thin by repeating the same people year after year. She pressed for the opportunity to make room for "a pent-up generation of poets even younger than the so-called 'young poets,'" who, she wryly commented, "might be anybody Robert Frost's junior."

But to the YMHA's regular audience, and many older members of its staff, the new poetry, much of it in free verse, seemed raw, undignified, and vulgar. They preferred the formal and more genteel style of an earlier generation. Tension over young poets was such that in the early 1970s, when I started receiving invitations to read from my work, I would report to a college or library and find hosts who were glad to explain to me that American poetry had ended with Robert Frost, or perhaps Marianne Moore. More than ten years earlier, when Betty had begun her "Introductions" series at the Y, the intergenerational battles reached a fever pitch. In many ways, they represented a conflict between the nineteenth century and the twentieth. The favorite poet of Dr. William Kolodney, for example, the director of the Y's education department, which housed the Poetry Center, was Edwin Arlington Robinson.

Kolodney had long been an advocate for poetry at the Y. He had to scrounge for funding every year, because the reading series did not draw the substantial audiences who supported the music, theater, and dance programs. Betty's "Introductions" presented an additional dilemma. Sponsoring readings by new, unknown poets was not feasible without a subsidy, but since Betty was willing to approach the Rockefeller Foundation for funding, Kolodney allowed her to proceed. He was wary of the young poets, however, and proposed to Betty that the Y appoint an "editor" to select the poets and monitor their readings. Howard Moss, one of the poets Kolodney suggested for the job, told Betty that this would be a thankless task. He suggested a committee of established poets that would not meet, but offer recommendations, and Betty enlisted poets from across the country to recommend new poets whose work they had noticed in small magazines.

Betty made this advisory list public, and in a 1960 letter to Robert Hazel, inviting him to read with a poet Louis Simpson had recommended, Diane Wakoski, she described what she saw as the benefits of the system. She admitted that she did not know Diane's work, but said that "Louis finds her gifted, and asks that she be given a hearing. One of the rules I have instituted here . . . is that poets (a different group each year) choose the young poets, and good earth is turned up this way." Today, even a partial list of the "Introductions" readers is impressive: Daniel Berrigan, Robert Bly, James Dickey, Edward Dorn, Alan Dugan, Robert Duncan, Lawrence Ferlinghetti, George Garrett, Barbara Gibbs, Barbara Howe, Richard Hugo, David Ignatow, Donald Justice, X. J. Kennedy, Galway Kinnell, Carolyn Kizer, John Logan, Frank O'Hara, Anne Sexton, William Stafford, Ruth Stone, Mona Van Duyn, David Wagoner, James Wright.

It was soon apparent that the younger poets were not always to Kolodney's liking. A 1961 reading by Robert Creeley and Paul Blackburn particularly offended him. Betty described the evening in a letter to Denise Levertov: "Kolodney thinks American poetry ended with Robinson. He and I were struggling all year over the question of 'ugliness' and eroticism in poetry, and we came to blows over Creeley. . . . [Kolodney] kept commenting, in a loud voice, all during the reading that the poems were 'unfit.'" Betty concluded that "the fact that poetry isn't safe works against it in this institutional age." Betty Kray and William Kolodney did share a love of poetry based on the belief that it exalts human language and gives integrity to ordinary experience. But they held radically different views of how a new generation of poets might fulfill this promise. Betty told Stanley Kunitz that Kolodney had become so disaffected with her and the series that she had the feeling he was watching her every move.

The 1960–1961 YMHA Poetry Center roster included many of the regulars—Auden, Eliot, MacLeish, and Moore—and the young Norman Mailer, whose World War II novel *The Naked and the Dead* had made him a literary sensation. But Kolodney was so upset by Mailer's reading in February 1961 that he pulled the curtain down in the middle of the performance—an act that received notice in *The New York Times*, the *New York Herald Tribune*, and the Newark *Star-Ledger*. I suspect that Kolodney had been ill at ease to start with, as the reading, set long in advance, was Mailer's first public appearance since he had been arrested for stabbing his wife and was set free on $2,500 bail. Some of the seven hundred who came to hear him had been drawn not by his writing but by his new notoriety.

Mailer began the evening by reading passages of prose. But then, according to the *Times*, he prefaced a long poem with a warning to the audience that anyone who found sexual imagery offensive might wish to leave. No one did. Instead, the audience responded to the poem with laughter. And Kolodney, as he later told the *Times*, was horrified that "people were laughing the way they do at dirty jokes in smoking cars." Wishing, he said, to "end a recital of . . . obscene images and vocabulary which broke the limits of good taste, and was not literature," he drew the curtain on what seemed to him the desecration of a place he regarded as a sacred haven for the arts (he had once told an interviewer that he hoped to attract to the Y "the very few persons in New York to whom poetry offers the theological, the ethical, and the aesthetic equivalents of traditional religion"). A newspaper editorial on the Mailer fracas concluded that perhaps both the writer and his audience "should be thankful that people still react, however wrongly, to words."

For Kolodney, the evening and the attendant publicity were personally devastating. The stage was set for Betty's exit from the Y during the next year, when Kolodney campaigned to deny the poet Frederick Seidel a first-book award that a panel of judges appointed by the Poetry Center, W. H. Auden, Louise Bogan, and Stanley Kunitz, had voted to give him. Kolodney first told Betty that a member of the YMHA board had found what he thought was an anti-Semitic slur in a passage about the Emperor Hadrian. Kolodney submitted the manuscript to the Y's attorney, who found a libelous reference to the archbishop of New York, Cardinal Spellman, as well. The real offense seemed to center on what Kolodney and others had determined were homosexual overtones in the work. Kolodney did not want to sacrifice, for a single book, the Poetry Center he had spent years developing; Betty stood firm on the principle that the institution should stand behind the decision of its publicly announced panel of judges, and not acquiesce to anonymous objectors behind the scenes.

The award was never given. Atheneum published Seidel's book without legal difficulties, and Betty, after resigning from the Y, spent the summer of 1962 traveling with her husband, who had obtained a grant to compose and promote electronic music in Europe. She was able to enjoy the beauties of the Rockefeller Foundation's retreat at Bellagio, in Italy, while considering an offer from Marie Bullock to be the first executive director of the Academy of American Poets. Betty hoped that the position would afford her considerable autonomy, but she was apprehensive. The Academy's newsletter, *Poetry Pilot*, then featured cute mottos, such as "Poetry says it best," and was adorned, as was the institution's letterhead, with a lumpy blue Pegasus. Betty arrived in this insular world not as a breath but as a blast of fresh air. And for years she campaigned—unsuccessfully—to get rid of Pegasus. She wrote to a friend in 1962, "I am trying to stuff all kinds of activities under the Academy's wings. If a reading program goes through, then that poor blue horse will look like a broody hen."

Betty did get her reading series, and much more. She and Marie Bullock considered how they might fund new programs and literary awards, including what became the first prize competition open to American poets for verse translations. They developed a proposal to install a national poetry library at the new Lincoln Center, a project that though it unfortunately never materialized, did establish their working relationship. Stanley Kunitz termed this partnership, which endured for more than twenty years, "the most formidable and irresistible twosome imaginable on the side of the angels."

Betty reassured Frederick Seidel that the showdown at the Y had been inevitable, and in no way reflected on him or his work. Moreover, she wrote him, "I'm very grateful to you that my resignation came on behalf of such a splendid book." In 1979 she was pleased that his second book, *Sunrise,* was selected by another panel of judges, William Harmon, Maxine Kumin, and Charles Wright, to receive the Academy's Lamont award.

The Relief of Hearing Language

It is difficult for me to imagine how alone Betty Kray must have felt when trying to impress on large philanthropic institutions the importance of the poetry that had surfaced in America during the postwar period. In February 1960, after a tense meeting at the Rockefeller

Foundation, she wrote an anguished letter to a friend, the poet William Meredith, describing how upon leaving the building she had darted into a phone booth on Sixth Avenue, where she could weep without attracting notice. "I am cleaned and plucked . . .

> *told that I haven't "the conception" (kindly, but patronizingly said, as one would say "she can't see the woods for the trees"). . . . I am told that I don't distinguish poets from poetry. . . . I do not define the power of poetry. I cannot say what poetry will do for the country, for the people, for the student. What is the state of poetry in this country? It is not enough to say it is a "high art." One says this nowadays about everything: salesmanship, advertising, interior decorating. One must distinguish poetry from other things. They need to know these things first, and then know what I intend to do about them. They would like to help support poetry, but I have shown them no means and no reason for doing so. I must think it over and get back to them.*

More reflectively, she added, "When they accuse me of not knowing what I want they are quite wrong, but if they say I am disoriented, confused, disorganized and overwhelmed about how to express what I want so that it is acceptable to them, the givers of money, they are right."

Betty went on to relate her frustration at being interrogated by six men who thought of poetry as soft and romantic, and took umbrage when she maintained that it is "virile, resilient, dangerously potent, and as enduring as the cockroach." She lamented that "we live in a time and in a country in which people don't think much about language . . . but if you say you are trying to open children up to language and unlock the way to self-articulation [and] don't use a lot of psychological terminology they think you are talking mysticism." She enlisted Meredith and other distinguished poets to help her prepare a grant proposal that would stand a better chance of allowing her to expand the national poetry-reading circuits she had painstakingly assembled. The title of the document she submitted to the Rockefeller Foundation reveals what she was up against, and seems absurd today: "An Explanation, Definition, and Defense of the Practice of Reading Poetry Aloud to the Public." It begins quietly, affirming that "poetry readings are spoken to a minority. Poetry is a low voice speaking in the midst of loud voices."

Grant proposals do not often make for stimulating reading, but most are not fueled by Betty Kray's passion. "Those who come to poetry readings come for relief, and for pleasure," she wrote, "especially the pleasure of . . . hearing spoken language in its most subtle form. I should say that poetry readings primarily serve the person who finds delight in language." She homed in on the importance of allowing people to "experience the oral imprint of poetry," and concluded that even the physical presence of the poet was important, for he or she is "presenting the flesh and bones behind the poem." The living poet "prevents the listener from abstracting the poem away from the living language and the feeling person, as is so often the student's habit. The spoken poem ceases to be 'ready made,'" refuses to be an object that exists to be manipulated, but asserts itself as something far more complex. The poem offered at a reading, Betty believed, was an experience as broad and contradictory, and as full of potential, as any human experience.

Above all, Kray wrote, "whatever results from the confrontation of poet and audience, there remains the intractability of the poem." Like a living organism, "it flourishes through time and change." In response to the officials at the Rockefeller Foundation who wondered what would justify their continued investment in poetry, Betty said that she regarded the hearing of verse as training the ear to appreciate what is best in one's own language. Ultimately, though, "this service, which invests the ear with a sense of discrimination and beauty, rewards itself. Art serves social good only by perpetuating its own appreciation and practice, and those whose ears are trained will want to encourage the practice of writing, hearing and reading poetry." While she didn't believe that the poetry reading could ever "serve a gross educative function," she dared to hope that the increasing interest in poetry among the young might help American poets to "keep the language alive for the next generation."

WOOLGATHERING

I was taken aback when James Merrill once asked me if Betty was as scatterbrained as she seemed. My only possible answer was: Yes, and no. While Betty was thoughtful and articulate, she was not necessarily direct. Trudy Kramer, who worked for the City Parks Department, has told me she regarded this as a subtle strategy on Betty's part, but people were often confused by her desultory style. And Betty did have a loose sense of time and place. One day not long after I began working for her, she rushed out of her office, frantic because we had a grant meeting at a foundation that afternoon and she couldn't find her copy of the proposal we were to make. Presented with this mystery—she had never asked me to prepare such a proposal—I went to her cluttered desk and found her current appointment book. In searching for it she had managed to unearth her calendar for the previous year.

A comment Betty made about the poet George Oppen and his wife, Mary, might serve as a description of Betty's own conversational style, and reveal why so many writers were at ease with her, even if, like Merrill, they sometimes felt at sea. "Yesterday I spent the afternoon at George and Mary Oppen's house," she wrote a friend. "They are leisurely folk and do not hurry conversation toward some intellectual destiny. I find that thoughts rise easily in their presence and nobody seems compelled to pound and knead them into an acceptable shape but lets them float about like pipe smoke." Betty was well aware that the drift of her own thoughts was easily misconstrued. When she heard that Elizabeth Bishop was annoyed over an offhand remark Betty had made about Bishop's appearance at Robert Lowell's funeral, she tried to explain herself in a letter that most likely was never sent. "A necessary quality of the funeral ritual for me is that it be flawed," she wrote, and said that she had looked in vain for this solace amid the suffocating "priestly aestheticism on display." She had desired "a humdrum funeral service inobtrusive enough to let the tensions and climaxes of feeling free themselves," a matter-of-fact setting that would enhance the beauty of the words of the Book of Common Prayer, and when she gazed around the church she was relieved to find Bishop "looking weary, thoughtful, a slightly disheveled woman amid the male pomp . . . [an] island around which all that flow of language would have to divide. . . . So that is what I meant. I wasn't talking about your hairdo."

Betty Kray was what my grandmothers would have called a woolgatherer. Often she seemed to pluck her thoughts out of the air, a scrap here, a fragment there. But Betty's woolgathering was of the exalted sort, such that she persisted until she had woven a blanket capable of keeping a person warm. Despite her flighty manner, Betty got things done. She was a dreamer, but also a practical person who consistently made her dreams—especially those involving poets and poetry—a reality. Her attention to detail never flagged. And she was deeply curious about other people, in a gentle yet persistent way that I admired.

I so often found myself incapable of good conversation, of asking the questions that would draw people out, that I marveled at the way in which Betty engaged people, not only asking intelligent questions, but listening well when they responded. Betty's ordinary conversations with poets were avenues to extraordinary events. Poets knew of Betty's long-term interest in translation, for instance, and James Wright piqued her curiosity by telling her how English renderings of classical Chinese poems had influenced his work, their spare but resonant style helping him embrace a less ornate poetic diction. Betty was a friend of the distinguished translator David Lattimore (when I accompanied her to his home in Rhode Island, he showed us the substantial Chinese–English dictionary that his grandfather, a missionary, had compiled in the late nineteenth century), and she asked him if he would be a consultant for a program she was devising, which would become a 1977 Academy symposium, "Chinese Poetry and the American Imagination." The panelists included Lattimore, several Chinese poets, calligraphers, and musicians, and a raft of American poets, including Wright, Stanley Kunitz, Kenneth Rexroth, and Gary Snyder.

Kunitz later remembered the important aspect of the event to him: "Poets and scholars got together, who had before lived in different dominions. We talked about the meaning of Chinese poetry, and found that we had a great deal in common." Gregory Orr was so energized by the event that he edited more than one hundred pages of transcripts from the symposium for an article that appeared in the literary journal *Ironwood*. Typically, Betty claimed nothing for herself. She credited James Wright; the conference, she said, had sprung out of his imagination.

INSPIRED READING

A born networker, Betty could not resist recommending to poets whatever good book she was reading, usually with such enthusiasm that they willingly took up the cause. The joy she had in discovering a good book was infectious, and few could resist. Betty loved Margaret Atwood's *Surfacing*, she told Denise Levertov, because Atwood "insists upon the necessity of the self to live fully and responsibly in an unglamorous, ugly world, an ordinary, everyday life. I've always thought that any person who did whatever he could with his life, and did this very well—to the limit—leaves his signature, like initials carved into the bottom of a hand-made chair." Denise, as a visitor to Betty's Rhode Island home, would have caught the reference to a sturdy old chair, one of many antique treasures that she had obtained for a song in the 1950s. Betty connected the chair's anonymous carpenter with Atwood's heroine, sensing they each had left "an imprint, anonymous but personal, something lasting, like the imprint of the anonymous sculptors on the wonderful statues at the portals of Chartres cathedral."

Flora Thompson's thoughtful memoir of a British hamlet early in the twentieth century, *Lark Rise to Candleford*, is one of "Betty's books" that has had an influence far beyond what she could have imagined when she lent it to me. Thompson describes the process by which rural people come to devalue handmade objects in favor of mass-produced items: how it is that a well-made but humble wooden table is relegated to the barn, or sold as junk, while flimsy manufactured furniture is purchased from a department store and proudly placed in the home. Years later, Thompson's chronicle of the way people in her hometown responded to the great social and economic upheavals of the period afforded me a reference point when I perceived the changes that were ravaging the area of the Great Plains where I had moved. It is one of the inspirations for my own book *Dakota*. In sorting Betty's papers after her death, I learned that I was only one of the writers to whom she had recommended Thompson's book; I found an enthusiastic response in a letter to Betty from Adrienne Rich.

I can trace the books Betty read in the early 1970s through the poems of writers who were close to her then. Another book she lent me was *The Bog People*, an account of how medieval corpses, evidently sacrificed in pagan rituals, had been found in Scandinavian bogs. Because of tannins in the bog waters, the bodies were often well preserved, so much so that the contents of their last meal could be ascertained. Jean Valentine, who had found the book through Betty, cited it in a preface to her poem "The Field," a meditation on the body in middle age: "Our breath comes shorter, / our lives have been a minute, a feather, our sex is chaff."

It was through Betty that several American poets discovered a memoir by the widow of the Russian poet Osip Mandelstam. Nadezhda Mandelstam's account of the brutal Stalin years, *Hope Against Hope*, inspired Jane Cooper to employ a line by the poet as an epigraph to her poem "Praise," which appeared in the collection *Scaffolding*. Cooper relates in her notes that she had first read the Mandelstam verse in this passage from his wife's memoir:

A woman who has come back after many years in the forced-labor camps tells me that she and her companions in misfortune always found comfort in the poetry, which, luckily, she knew by heart and was able to recite. They were particularly moved by some lines Mandelstam wrote as a young man: "But I love this poor earth, because I have not seen another."

Hope Against Hope taught me much about the ways in which dictators seek to control language. Nadezhda Mandelstam describes the civic atmosphere as so poisoned under Stalin that ordinary people were afraid to speak to one another. But I was struck also by the power of poetry to survive the machinations of tyrants. When it became too risky for her husband to commit his poems to paper, his wife committed them to memory, and long after Stalin was dead, she lived to see them published in English translation.

One book that Betty more or less commanded me to read was *The Autobiography of Malcolm X*, which she had recommended to Diane Wakoski and other poets. "I started reading it, I must confess, because I am interested in schoolchildren," she wrote Wakoski, "and the school librarians tell me that their libraries are being heavily patronized by black students, eager to read, eager to talk. It seemed the least I could do." The book placed her "in a world that I had denied myself," and she related it to a recent conversation with Wakoski. "This book threw me back to our discussion of the nature of loneliness. One finds the strain of loneliness, lovelessness, running through black writing, like ice streaks. They have felt it collectively."

As she handed me her well-worn copy, Betty explained that she had been moved by Malcolm X's account of how he had learned English in prison by reading the dictionary. His working vocabulary of just two hundred words had made him articulate enough as a street hustler, but when he first comprehended the vastness of the English language, he was astonished, and filled with elation. "Anyone who has read a great deal," he wrote, "can imagine the new world that opened. I had never been so truly free in my life."

I could see why Betty, who regarded language as a tool by which one might escape the confines of a provincial milieu, be it small town or urban neighborhood, the turf of the petty criminal, or the narrowness of ignorance, would have been attracted by this story. "Language is inseparable from behavior," she had insisted in applications for expanded funding for her programs aimed at public school students and teachers. "The young poets have established beyond doubt that children have desire as well as need for an adequate language, and we want to help their teachers convert this need into expression."

I sometimes felt that Betty regarded poets as a contentious family united only by its need to preserve the integrity of language, and her role was to pull the unlikely siblings together. She could see beyond differences of style to what would attract a young poet like Diane Wakoski to one unlike herself. She wrote to Wakoski, about Elizabeth Bishop: "One must sharpen one's ears to hear the wit; I notice that everybody does. Even the shouters quiet down to hear what's going on." When I made a snide remark about Robert Frost's so shamelessly basking in fame, Betty said that she remembered the old poet fondly. While he had to have sycophants, and the masses cheering him along, she found it forgivable, as success had come to him late in life.

Betty always urged poets toward community, one in which curiosity was encouraged rather than repressed, and wrestling with language might enlarge one's perspective on life itself. As for me, I had yet to contend with the language that would lead me beyond where I was at present. I had learned that poetry begins not in the chatty self-congratulation of the ego, but in silence. And it leads to a state of being in which we do not need words at all. My apprenticeship to this art would lead me into a period that, in its own way, was as rigorously pared down and solitary as that of any novitiate. It was also the loneliest year of my life.

Chapter Six

GRAVITY

I WAS A YOUNG WOMAN IN NEED OF GROUNDING.
The family life that had sustained me in my youth now seemed
part of a remote past, as did the church communities to which I
had belonged before entering the resolutely secular environment of
Bennington College. I had deemed the Christian religion useless
baggage, having no place in my sophisticated life. But I was aware
that I needed something, and the way I had been living, pursuing an
exotic nightlife and casual, one-night sexual encounters with friends,
no longer seemed the way to find it.

Having given up on a life in the demimonde, I tried something
equally extreme: sitting out the dance. I became increasingly withdrawn, slipping into a daily routine that was limited to bus rides to
and from work, and reading at home at night. I tackled *The Rise and*

Fall of the Third Reich, immersing myself in the horrors of Nazi Germany and surfacing to catch my breath when the reality of its evils became too much to bear. Between chapters I turned to other books for diversion, usually Betty's recommendations, George Eliot's *Daniel Deronda* and Charles Dickens's *Our Mutual Friend.* Soon, however, I would plunge back into the Reich. I kept at it for months, until I had finished the book.

My few social outings were usually related to my work, and this was a problem in itself. Other poets were often suspicious of the Academy, and by extension, suspicious of me. In the early 1970s the Academy had a confusing mix of blue-blood gentility and bold programs, reflecting the distinct worlds of Marie Bullock and Betty Kray. Because of its prominence, and perhaps the effrontery implicit in calling itself an "academy," it was frequently a target for complaint, and my social unease was greatly compounded by the fact that at any literary gathering I might be cornered and questioned sharply. Once a poet asked me why the Academy had excluded George Oppen and Charles Olson from its reading series. I knew that Olson had turned down Betty's invitations so often, at both the YMHA and the Academy, that she had finally offered him a perpetual rain check. And Oppen, a friend of Betty's, had once canceled a series of readings on her poetry circuits. This charge of deliberate neglect came not long after Betty had invited Oppen to read in the fall of 1973. He accepted, but a few months later, when we asked him to set a firm date so that we could prepare our annual brochure for the reading series, he backed out. As I attempted to explain all of this, I realized that, as was often the case in such situations, I was not getting through.

I decided it was not healthy that nearly all of my friends and acquaintances were other writers. Like many novice New Yorkers, I had attempted to create a smaller community within the city by associating with others of like interests. As a result, I dwelled in a small town, insular and self-absorbed. But many poets I encountered there, especially those who were close to Betty, were people I could admire. They appeared to have their writing lives in perspective, and had not allowed professional slights and resentments to harden into bitterness and suspicion. Somehow they held their egos in check and balanced the demands of their own creativity with their mentoring of students and other young artists. Jane Cooper, David Ignatow, Galway Kinnell, Jean Valentine, and James Wright, in particular, treated me with great hospitality, and a respect I felt I had done little to deserve. Even in casual conversation they often imparted great wisdom on the joys and demands of the writing life.

The Academy also gave me a chance to see the human side of poets I admired but could not count as friends. I had always thought Richard Howard, for instance, was like his poetry, elegant and aloof. But after his friend Adrienne Rich lost her husband to suicide, Howard offered to take over the class for teachers that she had been conducting for the Academy. And when he dropped by the office to talk with Betty, I glimpsed a warm and gracious person. He and Betty reminisced about having been teenagers in Ohio, and Howard spoke of the virtues of doing jury duty in Manhattan. He had been commissioned to do a new translation of Proust and had found the long waits at the courthouse ideal for the work. No phone calls, and few interruptions.

Howard made it clear that he was prepared to lead the class for as long as necessary, until Adrienne felt ready to return. He was exceptionally generous with the teachers in the class as well, speaking at length about a work-in-progress, later published as *Two-Part Inventions*. When he read his new poems, Betty and I, along with the teachers, appreciated the way Howard had rendered an imaginary conversation between Oscar Wilde and Walt Whitman, and adopted the personas of a host of Victorians, "even," as he said, with a grand flourish, "the Queen!" Several teachers later commented that Howard had given them a new idea: Why not have a student pretend to *be* Walt Whitman, if it would promote a better comprehension of the work?

While these older poets gave me something to admire and strive for, their openness and generosity belied what I was contending with in myself and frequently encountered in other writers of my own generation. I was more and more uneasy, not only with the jockeying for position and power, but with bad behavior that was justified as artistic license. The petty thievery that passed for youthful pranks—crashing parties and then making long-distance calls on the host's phone, picking pockets in Times Square, robbing the till at a "straight" job that one despised but that paid the rent— looked ugly a few years later. As at Bennington, I felt at odds with my peers, out of place, a hopelessly straitlaced, middle-class, and middle-western Nick Carraway who would never belong to the strange world in which I had landed.

I hoped that by becoming more reclusive I could think things over and work out whatever changes I needed in my life. But the sense that I could not afford to miss the next reading, film, or gallery opening nagged at me, and when I did emerge from my self-imposed exile, I was still much too careless for my own good. Easily distracted from a sensible course of action, I might, in a trice, succumb to such self-destructive and potentially disastrous impulses as picking up a joint from the sidewalk and taking it home to smoke with my roommate. Fortunately, all it contained was mediocre pot.

I preferred coasting through life to making decisions about how best to live it, and was incapable of commitment to any long-term relationship, except with Betty and the other women at work. I was usually able to perform my duties at the Academy as if nothing were wrong, and became adept at sustaining friendships in a superficial manner. This narrow, pinched existence was all I could handle at the time, and made me wonder if I would remain this lonely all my life.

I worked, without much success, on vaguely suicidal poems about the desire to evaporate like water on the surface of a windy lake. In some poems I identified with an aunt of mine who had killed herself in her twenties. Yet I was not willing to admit, even to myself, how confused and distressed I was. My relationship with Betty was one of very few anchors, the only friendship in which I felt exposed and yet secure. Through her mentoring I was being handed the keys to my own Doubting Castle. And like John Bunyan's pilgrim, I had only to recognize that the way out had been open to me all along.

One day Betty mentioned that she had met an interesting Austrian woman in her late sixties, who had studied with Jung and was now working out of her apartment as a therapist. She did handwriting analysis on the side to make ends meet. Betty, understanding better than I how much I needed direction, asked if she could bring the woman a sample of my writing from work. I was so impressed at the interpretation that resulted—the woman's having intuited not only my immaturity and confusion but also the fact that both my parents are musical—that I began seeing her for therapy.

Hannah was dignified, with an Old World manner, and her apartment felt as if it belonged in Vienna rather than New York. At our first session she asked me to start writing down my dreams. I told her that I rarely dreamed, and was sometimes afraid to fall asleep. But she insisted that I try, and that week I had such vivid dreams that I can still recall them nearly thirty years later. In one, I had rushed to catch an airplane but missed getting on, only to watch it crash and burn on takeoff. Hannah responded calmly, convincing my skeptical self that this was a promising start. She said that my unconscious was telling me to get back to earth.

Another dream involved a banquet hosted by a seductive, Circe-like figure. As I ate and drank, she changed me not into a pig but into an amoeba. Over the next few months, most of my dreams were about evil and its enticements. I was invited to the upper story of a deceptively appealing mansion, where doors opened onto roller coasters or a long fall to the ground. In one dream I returned to the mansion to find a party peopled by acquaintances from the literary world, who did not notice flames licking at the walls and snaking up a grand staircase. I was in an upstairs corridor, where I tried to prevent a malevolent presence from entering a room by blocking the door with my body. But it passed through me like a cold wind, and I ran for my life. At sunrise, as the great house was consumed by fire, I gathered with friends on the front lawn, in a rain reminiscent of the light showers of Hawaii, which coexist with sunlight and barely dampen the skin. Two enormous black birds appeared at the charred frame of a third-story window, then flew away.

HOT PANTS

I continued to see Hannah for half a year, and during that time the dreams I carried to her, and the work of pondering her nudges of interpretation, substituted for my poetry, as if this was all my muse could handle. It must have been clear to her, and to Betty, that the end of my love affair with the professor and premature success as a poet had left me with underlying insecurities and a generalized hostility of which I was still mostly unaware. I needed help. And hot pants were no help at all.

Those short shorts, in material ranging from silk to tweed, were all the rage in the early 1970s, and I was young and slim enough to wear them. When I received an invitation to a party given by Erica Jong, which I knew would be attended by many people I knew, I decided to wear a tight lacy blouse, scarlet velvet hot pants, and turquoise panty hose. I told myself that I simply wanted to see what would happen, how people, especially men, would react. My calculations did not take into account a very drunken Gregory Corso chasing me around a room, and a tense, chilly conversation with my former lover, who had come with a new girlfriend, another former student. A few of my friends seemed disoriented; apparently my outfit did not fit their image of me.

Late in the evening, when people were leaving, a successful middle-aged writer, a man I knew only slightly, proposed that I become his kept woman. I thought he was joking, but soon saw that he was making a serious offer. He would be able to set me up in a much nicer apartment, he said, and for a fleeting moment I thought of being able to afford sexy shoes at Henri Bendel. "Just think of all the time you'll have to write," he chided, his hand encircling my waist. If I live, I thought, slipping out of his grasp. As Joan Didion remarks in "Goodbye to All That," "It is distinctly possible to stay too long at the Fair." I went home from the party as I had arrived, alone.

Gerard Malanga remained in touch throughout this desolate year, and while I rarely turned down his invitations to a party or reading or the opening of a photography exhibit, I found it easy to forgo the late nights at Max's and other clubs. I remember him being excited about an afternoon reading he'd been asked to give at Halston's salon, and sounding scandalized when I said I'd never heard of the fashion designer. Gerard informed me that Halston had become well known in 1961 for creating the pillbox hat that Jacqueline Kennedy wore at her husband's inauguration. (The hat is also, more correctly, credited to Oleg Cassini.) By the early 1970s, Halston was designing clothing for a private clientele of society women who went for fittings at his atelier off Madison Avenue.

After Gerard explained all this to me, I asked him what I should wear. He suggested hot pants, as all the models at the event would be wearing them. Instead, I wore an ankle-length cotton dress with a smocked bodice and long sleeves. The reading was at a birthday party for Loulou de la Falaise, a young beauty who was a friend of Halston's and has now worked for many years as an inspiration and assistant to Yves Saint Laurent. The atmosphere at the party was stimulating but also disconcerting; I had seldom been in a room in which nearly everyone present was physically beautiful. Many models were there, including the incomparable, larger-than-life Naomi Sims, whose gusty laughter over a witty line of Gerard's verse I can still recall. I met the Warhol actor Candy Darling, whose manner was styled on Marilyn Monroe, and who moved more like a woman than any transvestite I have ever seen.

I had expected to find Halston intimidating and dismissive, especially since my dress was a $9.99 Indian import from a tacky store near Columbia University. But when Gerard introduced us, Halston's hospitable manner disarmed me. To my chagrin, he took an interest in my dress, particularly the smocking and the scalloped embroidery on the sleeves and hem. He seemed to think I'd done all right for myself on a limited budget. Or at least he made me feel that way.

I spent much of the party talking to one of Halston's models, a seventeen-year-old who had recently arrived in the city after graduating from high school in Cincinnati. Neither of us knew many people there, and we visited happily with each other. I had noticed her early, a cool-looking blonde who turned to me and asked, in an enthusiastic tone, "And what do you do?" Her smile was so dazzling that I was momentarily blinded, as if I'd looked into the sun. "I'm a poet," I replied. Clearly impressed, she said, "Oh my goodness, that's wonderful. I could never do anything like that." The adolescent gushing juxtaposed strangely with her physical hauteur; all I could think was to ask her about the literature she had studied in school. When I learned that she, like me, had latched on to Emily Dickinson, I said that this event at Halston's salon made me feel very much the kangaroo amid the beauty. And she confessed that her excitement over being in New York was accompanied by the fear that, having been given a chance at the big time, she would blow it and find herself skulking home to Ohio. Her striking beauty aside, she seemed an ordinary teenager.

As it happened, she remained with Halston and did very well as a model, one of the many people I met who became, as if by willing it, genuine New Yorkers. They had originally come from elsewhere, small towns or cities in the hinterlands, and they held on stubbornly in New York, working as studio musicians, museum curators, editors, actors, opera singers, and voice teachers when they could, and as waiters, strippers, taxi drivers, messengers, and office temps when the better jobs evaporated. I admired their ambition, and their air of having mastered the art of survival, landing rent-controlled apartments or good sublets. Any well-paying gig, such as appearing in an advertisement that provided residuals, could keep them going for months. I doubted that I had their nerve.

Some of them may still be in New York. The city does get into your blood. Life there is fast and driven and full of opportunity as in no other city in America, and when you live there long enough it can seem that there is no place to return to, nowhere you can go. I left after five years, having discovered that I had the nerve to move to my mother's hometown in South Dakota. My life was already pointing me in that direction, but it would be two years before I recognized that. I sensed only that I would never belong to New York as completely as Gerard, one of my few friends who was a native. Another was a writer who blew into my life in Gerard's wake and became an unwitting catalyst for my move west.

"To Kathy, Love, Jim"

Fast forward more than twenty-five years, to another place, the town in South Dakota where I live, and where I have spent the last five hours with two other women in the kitchen of our church, serving a post-funeral luncheon to more than a hundred family members and friends of a longtime congregant. Placing flatware, paper napkins, plastic glasses, and ceramic coffee cups on a dozen tables in the church basement; slapping butter and ham onto sliced buns; setting out a variety of donated salads (heavy on the Jell-O and mayonnaise, and this time of year, garden cucumbers and tomatoes); slicing dessert bars and cakes, and arranging them on large trays; estimating how much coffee to make, how many water pitchers to fill with ice. Just before the service is to begin, the funeral director comes downstairs with a head count, one forty-four, and suggests that we prepare food for two-thirds that many people.

We're too busy to go upstairs for the funeral service, and we can barely hear it on the downstairs speakers. As I put bowls filled with coffee creamer or sugar on the tables, I hear fragments of the Lord's Prayer, a reading from Genesis, a hearty tenor singing "Precious Lord, Take My Hand." After the committal service in the local cemetery, mourners return and pass through the lunch line. People I haven't seen for years, relatives and friends who have come to South Dakota for the funeral. We make more coffee, wash empty pans, refill the salad bowls. People linger, talking over second and third helpings. We make more coffee.

As the church basement begins to empty, and we see that we have more than enough food, we sit down to eat. Then the cleanup. My job is to clear the tables and scrub them with a well-worn soapy rag, and as I work, my mind wanders to my dusty house and the cleaning I have been engaged in there the last few days. Very early this morning, before I reported for duty at the church, I had finished organizing and shelving poetry anthologies, which had been stored in boxes for years. Then I started on our small collection of rare books, mostly volumes of poetry that my husband and I each began accumulating in college.

In one small pamphlet of poems, privately printed, I found a penciled inscription, "To Kathy, Love, Jim," which summoned for me a lanky presence in a small living room on West End Avenue: Jim Carroll, watching Knicks games on the black-and-white television that a college friend's parents had given me when they upgraded to a color set. Soured on sports since high school phys ed, where I was always the last one selected for any team, I knew little about basketball. But the New York Knicks were a big deal in the city, having won the NBA championship in 1970. In the 1972–1973 season, when Jim and I were watching games together, they were on their way to another championship. I still didn't pay attention, because Jim was far more interesting than the game.

Jim liked to talk, and he was good at it. He told me that winning a scholarship to an elite Catholic prep school had been his ticket out of an Irish ghetto and into early fame as an all-city high school basketball star. He spoke with great affection for the game, but also regret. Basketball might have become his life, he explained, but for the drug habit he'd picked up while experimenting with other kids, sniffing glue and guzzling powerful cough syrups to get a buzz. He hadn't liked drinking, and had confused the warnings he'd heard about drugs. Assuming that marijuana was the more dangerously addictive of the two, he began using heroin at age thirteen. At fifteen, he had done time at the Rikers Island juvenile reformatory for possession of heroin and drug paraphernalia.

When I met Jim, he was almost twenty, a few years younger than I. We were both Leos, but he looked the part: a memorable six-foot-two, with a mane of carrot-colored hair. He had begun hanging around St. Mark's-in-the-Bowery as a teenager, and credited those working in its Poetry Project, notably Ted Berrigan, with first encouraging him as a writer. Like basketball, poetry provided the discipline that Jim knew he needed if his life was not to spin out of control. For a time he worked as an assistant to the Poetry Project director, Anne Waldman. I had a more casual relationship with St. Mark's, but had admired Anne from the time when she was a few years ahead of me at Bennington. The easy self-assurance with which she identified herself as a poet had impressed me, and when I moved to New York I was glad to be pulled, however peripherally, into her orbit. I loved the parties that her mother, a delightful and urbane woman, gave at her Greenwich Village apartment. My own apartment, and those of most of my friends, had a transient air, but Mrs. Waldman's place felt like a real home, warm and welcoming.

I knew Jim casually, as another young artist in the city. Our work had appeared in *The World,* the literary journal of the Poetry Project, and in spin-off anthologies of verse from the magazine. We were both posed by Gerard Malanga for soulful black-and-white portraits that we later used on book jackets. And we attended many of the same literary events, most memorably a 1971 reading by Andrei Voznesensky at Town Hall. Betty had taken me because she wanted me to hear her old friend, and I was transfixed by a group that settled into seats near ours. It included Jim, the poets Allen Ginsberg, Peter Orlovsky, and Ed Sanders, whose band the Fugs I adored, as well as Bob Dylan. Betty recognized Ginsberg and went to speak to him. I was too in awe of Dylan's presence to follow.

When I got to know Jim, he was writing *The Basketball Diaries.* Several excerpts had been published, but he apparently needed to work the stories over by talking them out. Much of what is in the *Diaries* I first heard from him. I wondered at the time if he wasn't squandering his literary talent in telling his stories rather than writing them. And I worried that drugs would get the best of him, preventing him from finishing the book. I am glad to have been proven wrong on both counts.

Except for one wild night when we made love in the bushes of Riverside Park, our few evenings together were rather innocent. I would make popcorn, Jim would find the Knicks on TV, we'd settle in front of the set. And Jim would talk. And nod. I didn't understand how he could pay attention to the subtleties of a basketball game when he was semiconscious, but every now and then he would bounce out of a drugged stupor to comment knowingly on the action. Once, when I was sure he had fallen asleep, I reached over to remove from his hand a cigarette that had burned down almost to his fingers. Wearily he said, "Kathy, don't worry, I've been doing this for years," and took one last drag before putting it out.

I had never known a heroin addict, but Jim had a sweetness about him that overcame my unease. He did not shoot up in front of me, and I came to suspect that he appreciated my apartment as a refuge from the frenetic druggie world he has described so vividly in *The Basketball Diaries* and his journal of the early 1970s, *Forced Entries*. I had made a quiet place for myself, without a gang of people looking for the next party, the next fix. Jim appeared surprised that I knew so little about the "Dr. Feelgoods" then operating in Manhattan, medical doctors who regularly injected society and show biz clients with a potent mix of B-12, calcium, potassium, and pure amphetamine. And he seemed interested that I was not tempted to join them. In the argot of the addict, I had "virgin veins," and I intended to keep them that way. I had tried marijuana in college, but when I met Jim, I was using it less frequently, as I had decided that it hindered my writing. By the time cocaine was surfacing at literary parties, it was easy for me not to indulge. Friends told me that a cocaine high was much like speed, and that stopped me cold.

Drugs had a hold on Jim in a way I'd not seen before. He was looking for a way to get out from under heroin, and hoped that a methadone maintenance program would free him from what he has described as the "cockroach existence" of the junkie, always scrambling for the money to buy the next hit. Sitting on my bed, which also served as a sofa, Jim would talk about how much he hated the things he'd done for drug money; most recently, with Gerard

Malanga, he'd operated a gay porno movie house that Andy Warhol owned. When he was younger he had sometimes resorted to hustling homosexuals in public bathrooms or robbing people as they walked their dogs in Fort Tryon Park.

It felt strange to hear Jim say these things; his unsavory stories were at odds with the likable person relating them. Jim was remarkably good-humored, given his circumstances, and always impressed me as an essentially moral person, far more engaged in ethical concerns than many who were outwardly respectable but saw nothing wrong with backstabbing to advance their careers. Jim, for example, would not have done what I witnessed another writer doing; after a friend helped him obtain a part-time job on her college faculty, he spread rumors of her ill health in the hope of securing her more desirable full-time position.

Others recognized Jim Carroll's essential decency; the prominent artist who had hired him as an assistant trusted him to baby-sit his children. And that made sense to me. Jim knew what it was to be used, by drug dealers, by businessmen looking for a quick blow job, and by Andy Warhol, who loved to tape him over the phone when he was on a speed-induced talking jag but who would hang up if he called and found Jim sober. Having maintained a sense of himself despite the odds, Jim could respect the holy innocence of a child.

Jim, and Gerard Malanga too, for all the bad-boy behavior, had consciences formed in the Catholic Church, and where aesthetic values were concerned, they cast their choices in moral terms. Gerard, who had cofounded Andy Warhol's *Interview*, had envisioned it as a magazine featuring thoughtful discussions with a wide variety of artists and writers, and stunning photographs. But he left the publication when Warhol's obsession with commercial success began to make the publication stupefyingly trivial: out with the poets, in with the starlets and the Eurotrash! It wasn't long before the new editors were fawning over "celebrities" such as Imelda Marcos.

Jim Carroll and I met when we were both making important decisions about our writing that would lead to dramatic changes in our lives. Getting off heroin was, as Jim has said in *Forced Entries*, the "only choice for [his] work." He realized he needed "a consistency in my moods if there is to be any consistency in my style. I can't attempt to write always in the hollow flux of desperation and incipient terror."

Jim, for all his troubles, had the good sense to sit in a church and think things through. With all the churches in Manhattan, I am still baffled at my unwillingness to enter even one. I had loved to sing in choirs when I was a child, but my upbringing was such that by the time I was in my teens the physical elements of the faith had been heavily discounted. I lacked the basic knowledge of the value of a dark church lit by votive candles as a sanctuary where I might safely approach the questions that loomed large for me. In spiritual terms I had been left with literally no place to go. But Jim had what he called "the long church," which he had stumbled across in Manhattan, and its narrow shape was "somehow as soothing as its brilliant silence." In *Forced Entries*, he says he wondered whether it was only the silence that made him feel more lucid there, and then rejected the question as foolish; he was in desperate need of any clarity he could find.

In our own ways, Jim and I were each seeking more clarity in our lives, and beginning to make the choice to leave New York. We had long believed that being at the next hot cultural event, and the party following, was the most important thing in life. Jim once told an interviewer that he had to "break away from that as much as being around drugs, because that's a drug too." Encouraged by other writers from the St. Mark's Poetry Project who had fled Manhattan for Bolinas, a town near San Francisco, Jim went to his long church, lit a candle, and decided to leave. When I heard that he had gone, I felt the move might save his life; surely drugs would have killed him had he remained in New York. We had lost touch by then, but I wished him well. And now I knew that if a New York native like Jim could pack up and leave, I might do it too.

TUFF TURF

My own aesthetic choices in some ways paralleled Jim's. Like many young artists before and since, I had been bent on accumulating material for my work without much regard for the consequences. (The novelist Flannery O'Connor, a devout Roman Catholic, demonstrated considerable charity after being confronted at the Yaddo writers' colony with drunkenness and sexual license. "This is not sin," she commented, "but Experience.") And for a while New York City more than met my needs. I had found there, as Jim put it in *Forced Entries*, "enough external stimuli, enough experience, courtesy of New York City, to last a hundred years." It was time to move on.

But I didn't know where to go. Honolulu was not likely, and while rural Vermont attracted me, I dreaded the notion that I might become one of those people who hang around their former school because they never wanted to leave college in the first place. The possibility of moving to South Dakota was remote at best. Yet I did move there, in 1974, with a poet I had met in New York who not long afterward became my husband. When Jim's book was finally published by a small press in 1978, I bought *The Basketball Diaries*, rejoicing that he had been able to complete it. But it wasn't until 1985, in Jamestown, North Dakota, of all places, that I encountered Jim again. My husband, David, and I were driving home from Chicago and decided to stop for the night, saving the last 230 miles for the next day. We took a walk at dusk to stretch our legs, and when we passed a theater on the edge of downtown, I noticed a brightly lit poster for a movie entitled *Tuff Turf* and saw that it featured the Jim Carroll Band. "Oh my God," I exclaimed, "he's alive!" My road weariness notwithstanding, I insisted on seeing the film, which turned out to be a cheesy but enjoyable teen movie. I later read that a critic had termed it relentlessly brainless, but it was worth everything to me to see Jim looking all right, and singing his poetry to a hard rock beat. He had no more than a few minutes on film, yet it cheered me. The juxtaposition of the young actors' antics with the lyrics of "People Who Died," a litany of Jim's friends who had died of overdoses, murders, and suicides, was no stranger than the juxtaposition of Jim and me and Jamestown, North Dakota.

Every now and then my quiet life in South Dakota crashes up against my New York past. My husband and I will sometimes endure a silly film or TV show because we enjoy revisiting its Manhattan scenery, and I suspect that we have the only collection of Velvet Underground albums for many miles around. I once walked to the movie theater on Main Street just to see the Ramones in *Rock 'n' Roll High School*. The local teenagers in the audience, attracted by the title, were bemused by the film. Mostly the children of rancher friends, they had never heard of the Ramones and didn't get the S&M satire in Mary Woronov's role as school principal. Thirteen years before, she had appeared as a dominatrix in Andy Warhol's *Chelsea Girls*. It occurred to me that rural kids who had never come near the Long Island Expressway might not understand the phenomenon of the Ramones. Or Andy Warhol for that matter. They certainly didn't care. And I loved them for it.

Having seen *Tuff Turf*, I sought out Jim's first album, appropriately entitled *Catholic Boy*. His poetry was stronger than ever, and I was intrigued by one of the songs, "Wicked Gravity." When I met Jim, we were both trying to escape the demands of gravity by living in our heads. With contempt for what we saw as the drag of ordinary life, we had indulged in the dangerous folly of thinking we had found a better way. I was absorbed in writing cerebral verse about angels, and Jim sought inspiration in drug-induced hallucinatory dreams and nods. But we both believed enough in what Jim has called "the poem within" to let it save us. And it led us back to the real world, where, as the poet Meredith Carson reminds us, "Gravity is undone / by spider web and wing of butterfly."

Chapter

Seven

TAKING WING

IN THE FALL OF 1972 MY LIFE BEGAN TO OPEN
up. My good friend from college Andrea Dworkin returned from
Amsterdam, where she had been living, and roomed with me until
she found her own apartment in the East Village. For some time she
had been researching and writing her first prose book, *Woman Hating,* and as always, I was impressed by the way her mind worked over
an issue, in this case the pervasive presence of misogyny in world
cultures. Her chapter on Chinese foot-binding I found particularly
disturbing. In Honolulu, I had occasionally seen elderly Chinese
women hobbling along on stunted feet, but I had never comprehended the extreme cruelty of the practice. To create the ideal foot,
the toes were sometimes bent under so severely that they withered
and fell off. Andrea's keen analysis of this as an erotic practice made

me rethink the Charles Jourdan shoes I had admired in a store window and saved up to buy, only to find that the fashionably high heels made for difficult walking and painful arches and shins.

Andrea and I had met when I was a sophomore at Bennington and she had returned from a leave she took in 1965, after she had become notorious as the Bennington girl arrested in an anti–Vietnam War demonstration. After being imprisoned in the city's Women's House of Detention, she had forced a grand jury investigation of the conditions there. In many ways Andrea's feminism had begun then. It was not lost on her that the prison doctor who performed a gynecological exam on her while smoking a cigarette and without wearing gloves was accustomed to treating prostitutes with such contempt, but that only a middle-class college student would have the wherewithal to make her protest heard. Still, she was not prepared for the first question asked of her at the grand jury hearing: "Are you a virgin?" Andrea returned to Bennington while the grand jury continued its work, and ultimately the doctor and several prison administrators were forced out. She had hoped to continue her studies in peace, but after she refused an interview request from the New York *Daily News,* a reporter threatened to print photographs of her (taken with a telephoto lens) reading in her college room, and she fled. After some time in London, she settled on the island of Crete. She was taking a freighter back home, and would return to college in the fall of 1966.

Andrea had become a legend on the Bennington campus, and there was a hum of excitement in my dorm, Franklin House, when she was assigned a room there. We quickly became friends, and she later told me that she had been relieved to meet a girl from far-off Honolulu, who had never heard of her. We could be kids together, sitting in my dorm room singing along to Bob Dylan, or one of my favorites, the Shirelles' "Baby, It's You," or the Beatles' "This Boy." I have enjoyed many years of introducing Andrea to friends, who, having read her fiercely feminist writings, are invariably surprised to discover a shy, soft-spoken person whose wit and good humor make for excellent company.

The Coup Elephants

My friendship with Andrea developed because we recognized that the differences in our backgrounds and temperaments meant that we could learn a great deal from each other. I had come from a place where many of my classmates were Asian-American, so I was attuned to the considerable distinctions among Japanese, Chinese, Okinawan, Korean, and Filipino cultures. I had few Jewish friends, and Andrea was the first of my peers who talked to me about having lost aunts and uncles in the Holocaust. We were both members of the baby-boom generation, but World War II was past history for me, whereas for Andrea it had always been a presence in her household, an unseen but potent influence on every aspect of family life.

Andrea and I sought each other out because we both felt like misfits on the Bennington campus. I was a Navy brat, and arrived at the college in the fall of 1965 with an understanding of and a respect for the professional military that were highly unusual for that time and place. Most of my fellow students, including Andrea, had never known anyone raised in a military family, albeit an oddball one. The Navy music program had given my father the opportunity to work full-time as a musician while having a family, but as he likes to say, the only thing he ever killed was a little Mozart.

My acquaintances at Bennington were diverse, including debutantes from influential East Coast families as well as girls whose parents, members of the American Communist Party, had raised them in safe houses under assumed names during the Red Scare of the 1950s. All these girls could relate to the concept of my family as musical, with my mother teaching piano and my father playing cello in the Honolulu Symphony. But other things I learned to keep to myself, stories about growing up in Navy housing, or even the fact that my father had used his position as bandleader for the admiral of the Pacific Fleet to make a series of goodwill tours in Asia and Polynesia. His faith in folk music had been nurtured by presentations made by John Jacob Niles at Northwestern, and he taught reluctant Navy musicians folk songs from Hawaii, Samoa, Korea, and Japan. These songs frequently were the highlight of the concerts the band performed, as their audiences did not expect to hear uniformed Americans singing familiar songs in their own language. One day, on a rural road in South Korea, after the band's bus collided with a farm cart, my father staged an impromptu concert, converting what might have been an unpleasant situation into a songfest.

I generally responded to that inevitable 1960s question—Where were you when President Kennedy was assassinated?—by saying that I'd been in a boring French language lab. I told only a few friends that my father had been in Hiroshima with his Navy band that day, touring the atomic-bombing site and the Peace Museum. The musicians were in uniform, and many Japanese, openly weeping, had approached them to express their condolences on the loss of the president. My father was so shaken by this expression of sympathy that he left the group and sat by himself on the bus.

In the early 1960s, when the escalation of U.S. involvement in Vietnam was still largely invisible to most Americans—troops had not yet been sent, only steadily rising numbers of "advisors" to the army of South Vietnam—it was a palpable reality for anyone living near Pearl Harbor. One late-summer day in 1963 my mother and I were stuck in traffic on the Navy base, on our way to the exchange to buy school supplies. Bored, I tried to decipher the military acronyms stenciled on wooden crates in the truck ahead of us, and realized that the boxes had come from Vietnam. They contained the remains of American advisors being shipped home for burial.

Vietnamese ceramics were popular home decor in Hawaii, and one of our neighbors in military housing, who worked in Navy intelligence and often traveled on the admiral's staff, had offered to purchase some for us the next time he was in Vietnam. He was typically vague about when that might be. In early November 1963 he appeared at our door with a pair of brightly painted ceramic elephants that my mother had requested. Because they arrived just a day after the assassination of Vietnam's president, Ngo Dinh Diem, we dubbed them the "coup elephants."

Andrea Dworkin was one of the few people at Bennington to whom I confided such stories. I also told her about the disturbing flights that I took, as a military dependent, between Hickam Air Force Base in Honolulu and Travis, outside San Francisco. After my father's two years at the Navy School of Music in Virginia, my family returned to Hawaii, and I took advantage of this free trans-Pacific passage to cut the cost of flying to and from college. My parents would sign me up to go stand-by on a certain date, and I would wait for a call telling me when to report to the airfield. Occasionally I would fly on a windowless military transport, but more often the planes were sleek passenger jetliners indistinguishable from commercial aircraft, except that they carried the logo of the infamous

Flying Tiger lines, rumored to be a cover for the CIA. With other students bound for the U.S. mainland, I would board a flight that had originated in Bienhoa or Saigon, full of soldiers on leave. I will never forget how, along with the grievously wounded men in the bulkhead seats, the overtly healthy soldiers seemed damaged as well. They were mostly my age, but displayed none of the interest in the opposite sex one might expect; instead, they seemed to look right through me and the other college girls, as if we were not there. A young man, if he spoke to me at all, might admit that combat had left him afraid to visit his quiet hometown, because he would no longer know how to behave. One acknowledged a grudging respect for the war protesters at home; as he put it, at least they were reminding people that there was a war. He dreaded another visit with his family in which his attempts to talk about Vietnam would be met with an uneasy silence.

I could discuss such things with Andrea because, although she tended to comprehend the world in terms of politics, theories, and ideas, unlike many college students of the 1960s, she was not an ideologue. And while we were typical teenagers, able to sustain an unwarranted confidence in our own opinions, our friendship challenged us to make room for other points of view. We were an odd combination, the kid who had never even attempted to cut into the lunch line joining forces with the one who might try to unionize the cafeteria workers. But we were both interested in people's stories, and ultimately it was literature that bound us together. Andrea was one of the readers for the Bennington literary magazine *Silo*, and she still recalls the impact my poems made when I finally worked up the nerve to submit them. She and the other editors were surprised that a shy girl no one really knew was producing all this wild poetry, and were attracted by its energy and music, even if the meaning was often obscure. In Andrea, I found a friend whose prodigious reading both impressed and inspired me. The freshman literature course was one of the very few required classes at Bennington, but Andrea had been allowed to skip it after the professor learned she had read everything in his syllabus and much more.

Andrea and I came to enjoy the fact that we complemented each other—the optimist and the pessimist, the praiser and the lamenter, the poet and the philosopher—in ways that proved useful. I relied on her judgment when I was approached by the leader of a cult who had heard that I administered a small speaker's fund at the college. I agreed to look at his literature, which read like a Dale Carnegie manual for the soul, exalting the worst sort of manipulative behavior into a spiritual practice. I asked Andrea what I should do about this request, and after reading the tract, she suggested that I tell the man it was my policy to present speakers who were willing to submit to an open question-and-answer session after their talk. That was indeed the standard, if unspoken, practice on campus, and as Andrea had expected, the man refused these terms.

Bennington officials who were terrified of Andrea trusted me, and by conspiring against them, we got things done. After a class-mate (who, as I recall, was being scapegoated by the student government for various offenses—the true outrage being her flamboyant and unapologetic bisexuality) was threatened with expulsion for having a man in her room overnight—the rule against this was routinely disobeyed on the campus—it was my innocent face that got me the use of a copy machine in the administrative offices on a Saturday afternoon. The president of the college himself loaned me the key. Come Monday, he was presented with copies of a petition that Andrea had drafted, and I had duplicated, and that had been signed by nearly half of the students at Bennington. It stated that as they had had men in their rooms in the past, and would continue to do so, the college should expel them as well. My signature on this document was only partly a lie; I had not yet broken the rule but had every intention of doing so.

Andrea was one of the few people who could coax me into an occasional foray into Manhattan, a place that intimidated me, but which she knew well. I was forlorn when she arranged to complete her graduation requirements in absentia, and departed for Europe the summer before my senior year. In 1971, I used part of a writing grant I had received from the New York State Council on the Arts to visit her in Amsterdam. And the next year, I was glad to have her back in New York. She jolted me out of my lethargy.

SCATTERBRAINED

At Betty Kray's behest, I used another portion of my writing grant to take a month's unpaid leave from the Academy, and on my return she found me extra odd jobs designed to keep me involved with other people. The one I loved most was baby-sitting the energetic young children of Galway and Inez Kinnell in their messy but cheerful apartment in Westbeth, a newly established public housing development for artists and writers near the Hudson River. I liked children, yet except for one Bennington nonresident term spent as a kindergarten aide, I was seldom able to enjoy their company.

When James Wright told Betty he needed a typist for new work destined for a volume of his selected poems, she recommended me for the job. It began simply enough; on weekend afternoons I would go to the office to type and proofread. But only Wright's wife, Annie, was to know how I was progressing. She and Betty warned me that James might panic if he thought the work was nearing completion, and they instructed me to be vague if he asked how far along I was in the manuscript. Through this innocent subterfuge I came to understand that a dry spell like the one I had experienced after I finished my first book of poems was a common occurrence, and that to a writer, a looming publication date could be unwelcome, creating a sense of dejection.

One fringe benefit of the job was that it offered me a virtual seminar on Wright's poetry. When I made errors that couldn't be concealed with Liquid Paper, and had to retype a page or two, the repetition made me better appreciate the subtleties of Wright's rhyme schemes. Occasionally I would mention to Wright a poem that I liked, and he would launch into a story about what had inspired him to write it. Children he'd known growing up in a gritty Ohio River town, a teacher who had taken him to his first symphony concert, in Wheeling, West Virginia. Wright credited that experience with changing his life; he hadn't known that such beauty existed. Once awakened to the power of art, he had a means of envisioning and entering a world much larger than that defined by a high school diploma and factory job.

Ultimately, typing Wright's manuscript had consequences far greater than I could have imagined. I enjoyed pleasant meals with the Wrights in their apartment, and attended an occasional reading or dance performance with Annie. We got to know one another, and after James won the Pulitzer Prize for poetry in 1972, and the Wrights decided they could afford a long sojourn in Europe—Annie told me that it would be the only summer since he was a teenager when

James did not have to work—they asked me if I would like to sublet their rent-controlled apartment for six months. It was an irresistibly attractive offer—the chance to live alone, paying a lower rent in Yorkville, a good neighborhood within walking distance of my job at the Academy—and I told myself I was crazy not to respond with an immediate yes. But old apprehensions regarding New York City began to trouble me, and I would lie awake at night, weighing my options. The prospect of moving even my few possessions—one trunk, a brass floor lamp, two suitcases, my ancient typewriter, and several boxes of books—was daunting. I fretted over where I would go once the six months were up. The Wrights needed an answer, and I despaired of giving them one. One fine spring day, when I was walking to a bus stop near the Academy on Madison Avenue, I saw that the way through my impasse was right before me, but I had not wanted to recognize it, because it required a drastic change in my life, and a commitment I was not certain I was ready to make. With great trepidation, and a recklessness that surprises me to this day, I turned to my companion, a poet I had been dating steadily since meeting him a few months before, and asked if he wanted to move in with me.

Another poet had encouraged us to meet, commenting that we were both scatterbrained and would probably like each other. We had arranged a date after work in February 1973, on a night that turned out to be the coldest of the winter. As far as we were concerned, it was a vacation in the tropics, the most fun either of us had had in a long time. After drinks at the West End on Broadway, we had a leisurely dinner at a venerable student hangout, the Symposium on West 113th Street, near the Cathedral of St. John the Divine. Neither of us had expected much to come of the evening, as our poet friend was an oddball, known for acquiring peculiar acquaintances, including a prostitute he had once lived with and tried to reform. We were pleased to find ourselves engaged in hours of amicable talk about poetry, places, childhood, and family.

David was on the rebound from a failed marriage and a derailed academic career. Illness had forced him to resign from a teaching assistantship in classical Greek at the University of Chicago, and he had moved in with his widowed father in the northern New York suburbs. He was biding his time on the night shift at an industrial print shop, working presses that churned out business forms and airline tickets. I too had put my life on hold, and for the better part of a year had avoided dating, figuring that celibacy was better than casual sex with friends. But I began to feel I had lost the ability to love, as if the capacity had withered away inside me. Then, a few months before I met David, a good friend from Bennington, a gay dancer I had roomed with briefly when I first came to New York, had asked if I would have sex with him. He had started to doubt that he was gay, and I was the only woman he knew well enough to approach. I thought it over, and decided that was the least that a friend could do.

It is difficult now to recall the wanton innocence of that time, hovering between the sexual excesses of the 1960s and the onset of AIDS. My only worry—needless, as it turned out—was that a sexual involvement would mean the end of our long-standing friendship. We continued to go to movies and dance recitals, as we always had. The difference was that now we made love afterward. The sex was companionable enough, but I was longing for something more. The reawakening of my sexual energies had helped me feel alive again, but it was not enough.

SYNCHRONICITY

When I met David, everything fell into place. Our mutual attraction was such that we quickly became inseparable, spending nearly all our free time together. Betty, Dorothy, and Ellie had taken note of my infatuation, and when David first appeared at the Academy offices to pick me up for a date, he was aware that he was under close scrutiny. But he passed inspection and was made to feel welcome. He dropped by the office regularly, talking with my colleagues about books, films, recipes, and the quirks of the Academy's Manhattan neighborhood, which David knew well, having commuted from Westchester to high school at Regis, a few blocks away. He entertained us with stories of standing amid a group of schoolboys outside Greta Garbo's apartment building, hoping for a glimpse of her; of pooling money to purchase delicacies—tins of tiger meat, or chocolate-covered ants—from one of the gourmet shops on Madison Avenue; and of spending many lunch hours touring the Metropolitan Museum with a friend who later became a professor of art history.

Soon Betty was inviting us as a couple to Rhode Island. She liked David's verse, his extensive knowledge of the classics, and his love for the tradition of English poetry. She took us deep into the woods to visit a favorite holly tree, pointing out along the way the varieties of trees she and Vladimir had planted to attract different species of birds. David had spent his childhood summers camping in the Adirondacks, and he and Betty spoke with an easy familiarity about the ecology of northeastern forests. On one occasion, as we finished a simple al fresco lunch, Vladimir imitated the call of mockingbirds in a nearby mulberry tree. Then, to empty the tree of birds altogether, he made a noise that sounded alarmingly like a cat fight.

Later that afternoon, we went swimming at Moonstone Beach, then washed off the salt by plunging into a freshwater pond nearby. David's long hair was slicked back, and Betty got a better look at his face. "Why, he's a handsome man," she whispered, making me feel as if, in finding him, I had done something both adult and wise.

Our moving in together seemed inevitable, and as David's factory schedule was four days on, three days off, we had ample opportunity to get to know each other without being stifled by togetherness. The Wrights' apartment, a long and narrow ground-floor flat, was a good place for nurturing our relationship. We were fortunate to share access to a substantial backyard with a neighbor, an affable man who sang in the chorus of the Metropolitan Opera. I grew herbs for cooking, and David and I often read beneath a willow tree sustained by an underground stream that courses through that part of Yorkville. We fed the cats that stalked the wooden fences separating our backyard from others.

The building had originally been a tenement for immigrant workers, and signs of its humble origins were still in evidence. We had no bathroom, only a water closet at one end of the kitchen, and a tin shower stall that had been installed at the other. Yet to us it was the most romantic place imaginable, with every book that a poet could dream of, as well as the Wrights' collection of owls, represented in a multitude of drawings and sculptures and in decorations on everything from clocks to dish towels. The kitchen was small but well equipped. I cautiously attempted a few recipes from Annie's cookbooks, under David's expert guidance. He had learned to cook as a boy—it was how he avoided washing dishes—and on arriving home from work, I would often be greeted by the aroma of fresh scallops in white wine sauce, or David's homemade tomato sauce simmering on the stove.

Although we were barely conscious of it at the time, David and I were caught up in a great synchronicity, a constellating of circumstance that would guide our lives for years to come. We thought of ourselves as New Yorkers, David especially; as a teenager he had explored Manhattan daily after school, carefully calculating how many movies and soft drinks he could take in and still have subway and train fare back to Westchester. The idea of leaving the city was not appealing, and we were reluctant to admit that we had each turned onto a dead end there. But in 1973, the unforeseen death of my maternal grandmother in South Dakota offered us a way out. My mother did not want to sell the farmland, or auction off her parents' house, and David and I talked about moving into it until my mother could decide what to do with her inheritance. I had loved the house as a child visiting in the summers, and spoke enthusiastically of it to David. We would have more room, and because my mother was in no hurry to sell her inheritance, we could stay as long as we liked. My family would continue to lease most of the land to the ranchers who had been renting it, in some cases for several generations. It seemed a great adventure. The attorney handling my grandmother's estate suggested that we set up a family farm corporation, and I agreed to serve as president if I could name it. Thus Leaves of Grass, Inc., was born.

David was game to explore an unfamiliar part of the country, even more so when I explained that the western Dakotas are not flat, but consist of rolling grassland full of buttes, and badlands containing fossils of dinosaurs and prehistoric sea creatures. I sensed that my writing would benefit from the quiet of an isolated rural town, one in which I would be surrounded by family ghosts and childhood memories. Neither of us anticipated a permanent move.

Betty approved of this venture as a change that could inspire us as poets, and also help us build our commitment to each other away from the distractions of city life. Together, David and I made our plans. The Academy would look for someone to work part-time as a trainee, with the expectation that the job would become full-time once I departed in January 1974. David would give notice at his factory job so that he could start packing and shipping our belongings. January, I knew, would not be the best time to introduce David to the Dakotas, so we arranged to stay with my family in Hawaii over the winter.

David was thrilled at the prospect of seeing Honolulu. As a boy he had been fascinated by a yellowed newspaper photograph of Diamond Head that his maternal grandfather, a dispatcher at Grand Central Terminal, had kept in his office four floors below the city streets. His beloved grandfather had never made it to Honolulu, but David took to the place as if he were enjoying it for them both. Often he would take a city bus to the end of its route, and then walk back to where he'd started, becoming familiar with various neighborhoods in the process.

All that winter in Honolulu we lived off our savings, and my part-time income as an office temp. And we got to know each other. Having taken wing, we homed in on something neither of us had been ready to admit we needed. We began to build a marriage.

Chapter
Eight

" ONLY CONNECT "

I F IT WAS THE ILLUSION OF LOVE THAT SPURRED
my move to New York City after college, it was the real thing that
gave me the courage to leave. An everyday, warts-and-all love that,
without my noticing how it happened, became a marriage that has
endured for nearly twenty-five years. My tale may be the ordinary
one of an American woman coming of age in the latter part of the
twentieth century, yet it is also—and this is ordinary too—the story
of a transformation so profound that I doubt I would now recognize
the person I was at eighteen, or at twenty-six.

During my last year in New York, Betty Kray clearly felt that
I was on the right track and that, paradoxically, as I embraced one
change after another in the rapid flow of events, I was becoming
more stable. She did not believe that my leaving the city would mean

throwing away a promising literary career, but instead was convinced I would be forced to come to terms with my writing in a radically different way. Yet I was slow to articulate, even to myself, why I felt I needed to go. In the midst of sorting it out, I confided in a poet a few years older than I that I felt drawn to South Dakota. When he asked me why, I said that because my roots were there, I thought there might be a book for me out on the Plains. "Why?" he asked, in a skeptical tone. "Well," I replied, tentatively, feeling exposed and suddenly mindless, "maybe I'd write about my family." "Why?" he said again, more sarcastically. "What's so special about your family?"

He did not ask this in a teacherly manner, inviting me to serious reflection and response. His words were meant to silence me. I had learned not to flinch at the gratuitous cruelties writers commit upon one another, and the emergence of feminism in the late 1960s had made many people edgy. Some male writers resented any woman who presumed that she had a story, let alone that she was fit to write it.

But this man's casual contempt, while inexcusable, is not the full picture. If I take a hard look at the person I was then, I see that I had not given much evidence I would amount to anything, either as a writer or as a human being. I was naive, flighty, and often acted as if I had made a pact not to be present in my own life and could slip invisibly through others' lives without having any effect on them. This had allowed me to deny the pain I had caused another woman by having an affair with her husband. It also left me conveniently blind to the reality of the Academy's power in the world of poetry. I had taken refuge in my position as an underling there, glad to follow Betty's lead but unwilling to be held accountable for anything more than enjoying a wonderful postcollege job.

As I approached the age of twenty-five, however, I sensed that my refusal to accept responsibility for my life was making me more shallow than I wanted to be. It also meant that I could not take myself seriously as a writer. If other poets dismissed me as just another "arty" girl, the sort who writes verse in the protective environment of college but gives it up under the pressure of having to earn a living, they were merely following my lead. Their disdain was a bracing reminder that I had yet to develop my own voice. And in that sense it was a grace, which, after all, is merely something that merits gratitude. The word *gratuitous* comes from the same root.

And looking back, I am deeply grateful. I could not then have envisioned any aspect of what has become my life, not only the marriage, but remaining in South Dakota, and forgoing the security of a salary to enjoy (and sometimes endure) the scary independence of being a writer. I had yet to develop the instincts I would need to make many important choices based only on hunches. Betty Kray afforded me the opportunity to make the first of them, what I consider my first adult decision, because in thinking it through I realized that doing what I needed to do meant giving up what I thought I wanted. Having been set on an easy, well-marked path, I had to turn into a thicket of trees. And there, ignorant of the terrain and the extent of the forest, I would have to keep going, taking it on faith that I was pursuing the right course.

THE JOB

Betty had brought all this about by offering me her job. In the early 1970s, nearing her mid-fifties, she was envisioning another future for herself at the Academy, and began thinking out loud about how she might step down as executive director and devote time to developing special projects. I was but the first of several assistants she attempted to enlist in this scheme over the next ten years, sometimes acting with more wishful thinking than common sense. I believe she knew I was not ready to assume such a great responsibility, but floated the suggestion so that we could mull it over.

Betty's offer was attractive. I like to put down roots, and having settled at the Academy, I was eager to consider it a good place to stay. I enjoyed the readings, and being immersed in the planning and execution of a variety of programs with poets from around the world. But I also felt that I might be better off with another way of making a living. Over the years, when Betty and I had discussed my long-range plans, she often praised writers who had chosen professions unrelated to writers and writing. When my contemporary Laura Gilpin (whose first book of poems, *The Hocus-Pocus of the Universe*, later won the Academy's Walt Whitman Prize) began studying to become a nurse, Betty thought it a purposefully aesthetic decision, a "dive off the plateau of self-contemplation," where she saw many writers of my generation stagnating.

I was vaguely attracted to both library science and accounting, for the way that these disciplines impose order on chaos. But neither seemed right for me. Betty's offer did, yet as soon became clear, only as a spur to change. I had to admit that I had been marking time at the Academy, yet I wasn't sure that it was wise for a young poet—this young poet, at any rate—to take charge of the Academy's programs. When I spoke of my unease to the poet Diane Wakoski, ten years my senior and a model for me of how to be a poet with integrity, she said, firmly, that it all boiled down to how seriously I wanted to be taken as a writer. If I assumed Betty's position at the Academy, would I ever be able to trust fully in my poetic accomplishments? If someone were to give me a grant, or accept my poems for publication, would I always wonder whether it was because they respected my work or because they expected some favor in return?

Diane was expressing what I felt to be true, but hadn't wanted to face. And I had to admit that while Betty and I could have continued to work well together, and I would have been competent in the director's job, I would not have been more than that. I lacked the vision and innovative genius that permeated every program Betty touched. It was largely her efforts that had given the Academy such prominence. I felt that I was capable only of taking what she had created and running in place, which would have been fair to neither Betty nor the institution.

An innovator by nature, Betty was never happy with maintaining the status quo. The Lamont award for a first book of poems, for example, had been one of only two such prizes in the nation when Marie Bullock inaugurated it in 1953. But by the late 1960s, so many institutions were offering similar prizes that Betty felt the need to move on. Asking poets for their suggestions, she came up with the idea of using the Lamont to support older writers, who often had difficulty interesting publishers in a second book of verse.

Similarly, the poetry readings that Betty had struggled to fund in the 1950s were commonplace by the late 1960s. As she explained in a 1967 letter to her friend Robert Bly, she felt that the traditional reading—having poets read from their own work—had become stale and formulaic, largely a matter of writers' presenting their work to other writers. This signified a narrowing of vision that Betty found unacceptable, and with poetry readings "puffing up all over the place," she thought the Academy should offer programs "in the context of a continuing discussion."

As usual, Betty credited someone else with sparking her desire to change the ground on which poetry is heard. She was uneasy when the Swedish poet Tomas Tranströmer wanted to engage the audience in conversation after his reading, but she acquiesced, and later commented that while she had long disdained the practice of couching an artistic presentation in explanation, and hated question-and-answer sessions, she felt that Tranströmer had handled the discussion in a superb manner. Having decided the Academy was neglecting something important, she supplemented its annual reading series with programs in which poets would talk about where their poetry came from, and read from and discuss the work of obscure poets they admired or poets who had influenced their development as writers. In promoting a series entitled "The Education of a Poet," Betty handily disavowed the cult of self: "Since reading lies at the heart of a poet's learning," she stated, "the series will focus on books." Muriel Rukeyser inaugurated these programs, which included presentations by Sterling Brown, Donald Hall, Maxine Hong Kingston, Stanley Kunitz, Denise Levertov, Josephine Miles, and William Stafford.

Betty dovetailed the new offerings with the Academy's traditional reading series, so that a poet who was appearing in one might also appear in the other. Less formal presentations were made in the "Conversations" series, moderated in its first year by Jane Cooper. The series, described by Betty as "reading workshops for developing writers" of any age or professional accomplishment, engaged Maxine Kumin, Grace Paley, Alice Walker, and James Wright in dialogue with an audience interested in literature, its sources, disciplines, and methods. Betty's concept of a "reading workshop" was one in which, as she wrote to the poet and novelist Jim Harrison, writers such as he would talk to the group about "the kind of reading you used to develop in yourself as a writer, and the books which came into your life and fired up the writing process." Reading, to Betty, was essential to the making of a writer, and linked the writer and the reader as members of a community. Betty once enlisted the aid of nine poets, including June Jordan, Robert Lowell, Ishmael Reed, and Jean Valentine, who all lived in the district of a junior high school on Manhattan's West Side, to recommend to teachers books that might supplement the curriculum for the increasingly diverse student body. She told the poets: "We should like the community to know that a community of writers exists in their neighborhood and that these persons stand behind this program as advisors."

THE LITERARY CITY

In the mid-1970s, Betty tried to develop a sense of community among poets in New York by expanding the park readings that she had begun a few years earlier. From the start, these readings had been popular with poets. Betty wrote to a friend that at first she was surprised that "the poets are crazy to read in city parks, even for small sums of money... [even though] they have to read against traffic noises, movement, the distraction of dogs chasing flying frisbees." May Swenson commented that Betty had "invented a new way to make poetry part of the everyday scene in the city, to help it down off the platform and into the daylight." Swenson was pleased to find herself addressing an audience that consisted not of the usual suspects, but of New Yorkers who, "out of simple curiosity, would stop, approach, and listen."

I owe several of the best experiences of my life to these events. In May 1973, with the Parks Department staff helping navigate the municipal bureaucracy, the Academy arranged an event celebrating the ninetieth anniversary of the Brooklyn Bridge. The program began aboard the *Wavertree*, a nineteenth-century merchant marine schooner that had recently been moored by the new South Street Seaport Museum, where several writers read poems about the bridge by Elizabeth Bishop, Hart Crane, and Walt Whitman. The audience then boarded a city fireboat, borrowed in order to reinstate, for one glorious (and one-way) ride, the Brooklyn ferry that Walt Whitman had known so well. Once in Brooklyn, the group walked to the Long Island Historical Society, where Harvey Shapiro and Paul Zweig read more poems about the bridge by Yvan Goll, Vladimir Mayakovsky, George Oppen, and Louis Zukofsky. We then joined the crowds gathered on the promenade to see a municipal fireworks display and to sing "Happy Birthday."

Three things about the event stand out in my mind: the mountain of paperwork graciously handled by Trudy Kramer of the Parks Department staff, the pouring rain that failed to hamper our celebratory spirit, and James Wright's sonorous voice reading Whitman's "Crossing Brooklyn Ferry" as we crossed the East River:

> *I am with you, you men and women of a generation, or ever so*
> *   many generations hence,*
> *Just as you feel when you look on the river and sky, so I felt,*
> *Just as any of you is one of a living crowd, I was one of a crowd,*
> *Just as you are refresh'd by the gladness of the river and the bright*
> *   flow, I was refresh'd . . .*

As spectacular as that "ferry" ride was, I treasure my memory of another reading even more. One Sunday afternoon, the Academy sponsored a reading in Brooklyn Heights by Charles Reznikoff, then in his late seventies, and Harvey Shapiro. The Parks Department provided a lectern with a microphone, set up on the promenade. Shapiro has written, in a memoir of Reznikoff: "It was a sunny day and there were old people seated on the benches. . . . As Charles read, people gathered, just people strolling. . . . He seemed to be talking to them, and of course he was describing things they saw every day of their lives but never really saw, or never thought worth seeing, until this poet gave them back their streets and their lives."

Because it was an occasion for him, Reznikoff had worn a suit and tie. After the reading, he invited me to walk to Manhattan with him over the Brooklyn Bridge. As we strolled he spoke of having walked every day over many years to his work as a writer and editor for a legal reference firm. (I later learned that for most of his life he had covered nearly twenty miles a day on city streets.) He told me how good his life had been, with all the walking and the writing, and how important it was for a young poet like me to stay healthy. "The people I worked with are dead," he commented, adding with a sigh, "Of course, they smoked like chimneys, and drank a fifth of whiskey a day."

We both noticed that the air was exceptionally clear, and marveled at the distance we could see, all the way up to the southern edge of the Bronx. We stood awhile on the wooden walkway, and Reznikoff pointed to architectural details on Manhattan buildings, many of which, he said, were usually lost in the haze. I thought for a moment that Reznikoff had led us into a magical space which only seemed like New York, the city in glory. But the next morning I read in the *Times* that on the afternoon of Sunday, May 23, 1971, the air in New York City was the cleanest it had been since 1952, when the city's Air Resources Department had begun taking measurements.

As Betty expanded the parks readings, her assistants at the

Academy, myself and another young writer, Linda Sherwin, were her listening posts and co-conspirators. Not long after I departed in 1974, Betty's walks moved into the streets, becoming a distinguished series that over a ten-year period invited participants to take in New York's ecological, social, and even military history. One walk, which began on West Ninety-seventh Street, commemorated a "smart skirmish" of September 1776 and included a talk by the historian Bruce Bliven, readings of Revolutionary War–era poetry, and period wind music by the Federal Music Society. A naturalist led a tour through a part of Central Park that is still original forest, and for Inwood Park, at the northern tip of Manhattan, Betty arranged poetry readings accompanied by talks from an ecologist and a historian, who discussed the island in Indian and Dutch times.

Betty enlisted other institutions in the exploration of New York literary history. With the Museum of the City of New York she employed poets to present programs with scholars on such topics as nineteenth-century nursery rhymes, and the work of Maria Lowell, Jean Toomer, Stephen Crane, and H. Phelps Putnam. She commented dryly to a friend, "We presented dead American poets and got an audience." And she continued the series of historical walks: "Hart Crane's Village," led by his biographer John Unterecker; "Walt Whitman's Manhattan of the 1840s," presented by the biographer Gay Wilson Allen, the poet Galway Kinnell, and Marjorie Pearson, an architectural historian; "Langston Hughes's Harlem of 1926," with the scholar Nathan Huggins, and the poets Quincy Troupe and June Jordan; "Edgar Allan Poe as New York Journalist," with the biographer James Dillon and readings by Muriel Rukeyser. Betty incorporated the interests of contemporary poets as well. Nathan Whiting, for example, who had drawn inspiration from long walks at the industrial edges of the city, conducted a "Rivers, Docks, and Warehouses" walk that was so popular it had to be repeated.

"Only Connect"

As her series of walks continued, Betty grew wholeheartedly devoted to researching writers' lives in nineteenth-century New York City as a means of providing contemporary writers with an enhanced perspective of their own time and place. In 1978 she wrote to Galway Kinnell that this work was giving her a newly textured sense of life in the city. She observed that Herman Melville had "perfected himself as a poet" when he lived on East Twenty-sixth Street, and she imagined him watching the draft riots of 1863 from his rooftop.

Merrill Oliver, who worked at the Academy during this period, once said that Betty designed the walks to enhance the relationship of poet and audience, as people gathered around trees or on sidewalks, without the sense of distance provided by a stage. Betty wanted to help people make essential connections, to link the living writer with the literary ancestor by getting everyone out into the streets where Walt Whitman, Hart Crane, and Willa Cather had walked, while reading or listening to their words.

The waterfront edges of Manhattan particularly interested Betty, as they had been important to earlier writers, but by the early 1970s they were a wasteland glimpsed from highways overhead. In 1974, she asked Allen Ginsberg to give a reading at the South Street Seaport Museum, which was then struggling to survive as a nonprofit educational institution. And in her "Walk Through Melville's North River," she invited people to hear not only the words of

Melville and his contemporaries, but the poet Thomas Lux reading an entertaining account she had found of the noisy chaos of waterfront commerce in Melville's time. Listeners could try to imagine what Melville had seen as a boy, and recounted in his novel *Redburn:* "the coppered and copper-fastened" brigs, "black, sea-worn craft, with high, cozy bulwarks, and rakish masts and yards" rising above docks full of "musty bales and cases of silks and satins."

One of the books Betty passed on to many friends in the early 1970s was E. M. Forster's *Howards End.* The novel, published in 1910, had themes that seemed even more pertinent sixty years later: the countryside swallowed up by suburbs, tensions between hidebound men and newly emancipated women, and the hardening of class distinctions in a modern industrial society. I believe Betty saw its epigraph, "Only connect," as a moral imperative, and she intended to instill it as a value in those who worked with her.

But few people have Betty's ability for "only connecting," which I have come to see as her essence. Her ability to draw together people, places, and times, was nothing short of miraculous, especially for the callow poets such as myself whom she dragged around town. In researching the literary history of Chelsea, Betty became interested in the painters who had settled there early in the twentieth century, including Robert Henri and John Sloan, derogated as the "Ashcan School" for their realistic depictions of urban life. A similar revolution was stirring among writers, in the prose of Stephen Crane, Theodore Dreiser, and Upton Sinclair. Like the new generation of poets in the 1950s and 1960s, these artists were labeled coarse if not obscene by people of more traditional tastes, who felt that art should reflect only that which is noble and refined.

Enchanted by accounts of a boardinghouse where many writers and artists, including John Butler Yeats, father of the poet, had lived, Betty sought out the building. It had been run by three sisters from Brittany named Petipas, and the backyard dining area had served as the background for a Sloan painting, *Yeats at Petipas*, which counts in its jolly group of diners the writers Alan Seeger and Van Wyck Brooks. In a letter to Jane Cooper, Betty described visiting the Petipas building, at 317 West Twenty-ninth Street, relating that its superintendent had offered her and her assistant, Henri Cole, a tour. They also visited 165 West Twenty-third, where Sloan had moved in 1904, and happened to find a man "enamored of Stephen Crane," who offered to take them to the roof. Once there, Betty could tell she was standing where Sloan had once stood: he had "painted a picture from the roof and made a lot of etchings and drawings of various scenes he witnessed from that spot. Ecstasy."

Only in Betty's city could such things happen. Only in Betty's city could I converse at an Academy reception with the distinguished poet John Hall Wheelock, then well into his eighties, who had for many years been an editor at Scribner's, working with such authors as Thomas Wolfe, Louise Bogan, and Allen Tate. As Wheelock sipped a Manhattan, grateful that he could still enjoy a cocktail on occasion, we told him we were planning a program in which we hoped to take the audience on a ferry to Brooklyn. Betty's eyes lit up, and she said, "You must remember the Brooklyn ferry, John." Wheelock replied that his father had taken it every day to his job on Wall Street, and that he had always been thrilled when he was permitted a ride. "Once," he told us, "when I was very small, five or six years old, my father hoisted me to his shoulders and pointed to a dignified, white-haired man with a great beard. He was standing alone, his face to the wind. 'I want you to always remember this, John,' my father whispered in my ear. 'Remember that you have seen Mr. Whitman.'"

THE GREATER WORLD

Betty's "only connecting" did not stop at national borders; her international reputation was such that poets from abroad would often come to the Academy office, bearing letters of introduction from a translator or another writer. When that happened, Betty would drop what she was doing and invite the poet to lunch, coffee, or just a walk in Central Park. If I was lucky enough to tag along, I would get a crash course in history, and sometimes a new perspective on Manhattan. I will never forget the exile from Afghanistan who said that he was enjoying New York City much more than he had expected, as the skyscrapers reminded him of the mountains back home. Or the young Albanian poet, a Galatian by ancestry, who grimly predicted the bloody chaos that would grip the Balkans after the death of Tito. He feared that he and his family would one day be murdered or made refugees by people seeking revenge for past events and resentments that had festered for centuries. It was after our lunch with him that Betty lent me her copy of Rebecca West's *Black Lamb and Grey Falcon,* an account of a journey through Yugoslavia in 1938 which still stands as a good introduction to the tortured history of that region.

Betty had a way of engaging others in her ideas and affinities that had less to do with her personal magnetism than with the fact that over the years so many poets decided that what she found essential was essential to them as well. Her enthusiasms were not passing fancies, but reflected an abiding concern with the most profound implications of literature. No one who knew Betty would describe her as a patient person, but where poetry was concerned, she could allow time for the germination, gestation, and growth of an idea, until what had been a mere nudge of a question flowered into a communal pursuit, attracting writers to both self-examination and dialogue.

In the early 1960s, Betty began to read, in British periodicals, the emerging generation of African writing in English, Wole Soyinka, Chinua Achebe, and Kofi Awoonor. She wrote to Marie Bullock that "the literary level of [these] periodicals—and I hear the French are equally good—are so high that one blushes for these foolish little things published here." When she discovered that a group of African writers had been invited to a literary conference in Berlin in 1965, Betty hoped to bring them to the United States for readings in New York and on her national poetry circuits. But foundation grants were not forthcoming, and the State Department proved extremely reluctant to issue the writers the necessary visas.

Despite the setback, Betty kept hold of the idea that the Academy should take notice of the new global literature in English. In 1964 she invited the West Indian poet Derek Walcott to read in the Academy series at the Guggenheim Museum, and his presentation confirmed Betty's sense that the growth of a literature from writers in places as diverse as Nigeria, Australia, and the West Indies was a significant development. For years she kept her ears open, pestering poets and translators to help her devise a program, emphasizing that any such conference should focus on "the idea that instead of having one body of English literature we now have many. Not just American or British, but Caribbean, Australian, Canadian, Indian, and the anglophone literatures of tribal peoples." To Galway Kinnell, she wrote: "I should prefer to think that [V. S.] Naipaul, Kofi Awoonor, Derek Walcott, Nadine Gordimer, Les Murray, Margaret Atwood, and all the American poets are writing in the same language but somehow differently. I don't know how to express this in terms of a topic for a conference. Can you do it for me?"

When her conference was finally in sight, Betty enlisted Derek Walcott to give a lecture on West Indian poetry, and afterward told Kinnell that he had presented "a stunning essay in verse on the topic we had asked him to talk about, the imperial language and what the 'inferior' did to make it his own. It is eloquent. He made it possible to understand the process of making the language his own—and the anguish." Betty was pleased that the poems were to appear in *The New York Review of Books;* they later became a part of Walcott's book *The Fortunate Traveller.*

In late April 1980, a few months after Walcott's talk, the symposium that Betty had dreamed of for sixteen years finally took place, at Columbia University. It included Walcott, Kofi Awoonor, three Australian poets who were touring the United States, Vincent Buckley, David Malouf, and Les Murray; and the American poets Gregory Orr, Louis Simpson, Mark Strand, Shirley Williams, and Paul Zweig.

Betty had asked the conference participants to consider, among other questions, What sort of cultural burden will the English language carry? How much can it carry? These are questions that are of even greater importance in the twenty-first century, as people around the globe come to terms with the fact that the effects of colonialism are still very much with us. Betty said that the most moving part of the conference for her came when Walcott posed the question, "Is Caliban my ancestor?"

A Place for Poets

Throughout her lengthy career, Betty sought to provide poets with ample opportunity to consider such vital questions. And she valued New York City's drawing power, simply because it helped her bring poets together. In June 1966, when Paul Blackburn informed Betty that the Chilean poet Pablo Neruda would be visiting the city, she asked Blackburn to arrange a gathering of writers from Chile, Mexico, and the United States so that Neruda could read his poetry and discuss translation. They met in Betty's living room.

In 1971, four years after Betty had asked Gary Snyder to suggest the names of Japanese poets the Academy might bring to the United States for a tour, she was able to welcome Tuzuru Katagiri, Ryuichi Tamura, and Shuntaro Tanikawa to an informal supper in her apartment. They had spent a day recovering from their long flight, and Betty felt they needed a home-cooked meal. I helped her carry the groceries from a market near Columbia, and that evening enjoyed listening to the poets, their translators, and several American poets they had expressed an interest in meeting talk poetry and history. The eldest of the three, Shuntaro Tanikawa, who had served in the Japanese navy during World War II, spoke of poetry as a language transcending national boundaries, a perception he had come to while reading the poetry of Auden and Eliot aboard his ship. He was forced to ask himself why his country was at war with theirs.

Betty had long wanted American poets, New York residents as well as those passing through, to have a space where they could gather to read, work, and have informal discussions. She had hoped that the Academy could provide such a place, but Marie Bullock had not been successful in prevailing on her wealthy friends to help her acquire a suitable Manhattan property. Betty came to see that the Academy could not sustain the kind of space she envisioned, and in the mid-1970s she approached Stanley Kunitz and Gerald Freund, who had helped steer grant proposals through the Rockefeller Foundation in the 1950s, asking them to help her brainstorm what Kunitz has described as "an idea for establishing a library to meet the specific needs of poets, including a comfortable reading and work space. London and Paris had recognized the need for such a facility, but not the city that was presumably the poetry capital of the United States."

Betty originally dropped this idea on Kunitz out of the blue. She had gone to his apartment to ask if he thought it would be feasible to found such a place as an independent institution. All she had was the concept, and Stanley supplied the name, "Poets House," which he and Betty felt would convey a sense of hospitality. As she was leaving, she turned to him at the door and said, "Of course, Stanley, you will have to be president." Kunitz, who had been involved with every one of Betty's programs since they met in the early 1950s, stated at her funeral that she "was forever dreaming up wonderful new projects. I am tempted to paraphrase what Keats said of Adam: She awoke and found her dream was true. But that would be misleading, and discount the hours of labor Betty put in—writing grant proposals, drumming up support, banging at the appropriate doors. In the end, she always had her way. No one could resist her."

Gerald Freund recalled with fondness the initial meetings of the fledgling organization. "Our first gathering was in someone's loft," he said, "with about twenty-five people, all believers in Betty's new project." She wanted to proceed cautiously, and for several years, Freund said, "all we did was plan, and solve the problems that arose, with Betty in the thick of it." Betty was determined to create an institution that would be run by poets in a democratic manner, not subject to any one clique or school. She gathered statements from friends in support of her proposal. Derek Walcott wrote, "For the young writer coming to New York . . . there is no gathering place at present that offers him the warmth of exchange with his peers. When I came to New York almost thirty years ago, I often imagined such a place." Armand Schwerner hoped that Poets House would "provide a little refuge from separateness . . . a useful home for the vaguely connected, the loyally opposed, the lovers of talk, the empathetically silent . . . a place for the members of what the late Paul Blackburn used to call the Republic of Poetry."

Poets House was incorporated in 1985, after $10,000 in grant money came from an anonymous donor who knew of Betty's track record in the arts. Soon after, poets began donating books. The first large collection was from the estate of Paul Zweig. Betty intended that one of the functions of the Poets House library would be "to gather fugitive materials such as [small-press books], magazines, chapbooks, and other ephemeral publications," without which poets and scholars would find it "impossible to re-create the sense of a literary epoch." When she knew she was dying, Betty made it clear that she wanted her own poetry books to be sold to raise funds for Poets House, and in the summer of 1987 she supervised my packing of this collection, which included annotated page proofs of Auden's "September 1, 1939," and versions of Galway Kinnell's "The River" with handwritten revisions. Everything went into boxes that the first director of Poets House, Rachel Bellow, helped me take to rooms in a high school that Betty had negotiated, enlisting the aid of old friends on the New York City Board of Education. In exchange for the space, Poets House offered programs for high school students and teachers.

Stripping Betty's bookshelves of volumes that had become familiar to me over the years spoke of a stark finality, but I could not help sharing Betty's joy in what for her was the realization of a dream. She had begun working on behalf of poets in 1954, and for thirty-three years had wanted to offer writers a place of their own, an open house with room for a library, and work stalls, and a meeting space that would contribute to a sense of community.

In the 1950s, Betty's office at the YMHA had been a mirrored dressing room behind the stage. Even in those cramped surroundings, she had managed to convey to poets that they were a part of something spacious and grand. Stanley Kunitz, who often introduced the young poets Betty had invited to read, recalls William Stafford's appearance: He was "terribly nervous. I think he'd never been east of the Mississippi. He'd certainly never been to New York, and was terrified of the big city, but excited about reading at the Y. Betty calmed him down. She always did everything in her power to make poets from the most distant parts of the country feel that they belonged—that theirs was the greater world of poetry."

Chapter

Nine

SOLICITUDE

❧

THE FIRST TIME THAT I STAYED WITH THE
Ussachevskys, during the spring of my senior year in college,
I was glad to accept their offer of a place to spend a weekend in the
city. I soon learned, however, that I was sharing the small guest room
with stacks of papers and files, some of which I had to remove from
the bed in order to settle in for the night. When I asked Betty where
to put them, she said, distractedly, "Just anyplace—on the floor." I
objected, as some of the letters were handwritten notes from W. H.
Auden and I thought they deserved better treatment. "They're just
about his rent," she replied, "and his nutty tenant." She explained
that years before, when he was planning an extended stay in Europe, Auden had given her power of attorney over his financial affairs. She had been responsible for paying his rent on St. Mark's

Place, and also collecting rent from a subletter. The chaos in the room vividly illustrated a mood of Betty's I came to know well: a consuming desire to impose order—once and for all—on her papers, and on her life. But when she had begun the process, she would be interrupted so often that the result was always a greater disorder than before. The chaos of papers and files in the guest room was a monument to many previous attempts to organize: manila folders neatly labeled but empty, sheets of adhesive dots that were evidently meant for a color-coded filing system, long since abandoned. All of it was oddly welcoming; I felt at home, and also blessed by the presence of Auden's blue scribblings on onionskin.

I had to laugh when, in sorting through Betty's papers after her death, I found many letters that might be paraphrased as: "Do you remember me? You invited me to read from my first book five years ago, and I slept in your back room for a week." In 1962, Betty wrote plaintively to Richard Hugo, who had asked for help in finding a place to stay when he came to read for the Academy, "We lost our hostel for poets when Robert Bly moved out of town"; her unsuccessful attempts to find lodging for Hugo with Academy patrons led her to conclude that "rich people like to put up the English poets." Betty's solution was to start using her own apartment.

The position of Betty's husband at Columbia, where he had co-founded the renowned Columbia–Princeton Electronic Music Center, assured the Ussachevskys of a rent-subsidized apartment near the university. When I first met them they lived on Morningside Drive, and their neighbors included Arthur Miller and his wife, Marilyn Monroe. Betty, unfamiliar with Monroe's films, recalled her as a shy woman who had come to a party on a muggy summer day looking miserable in a tight dress and heavy makeup that dissolved in the heat. The Ussachevskys later moved to a larger apartment on

Claremont Avenue, near 116th Street, that included a former maid's quarters—a narrow bedroom and bath off the kitchen. While Betty longed to turn this space into an office for herself, she also felt compelled to offer hospitality.

She did not think of herself as a maternal person, but housing and feeding people gave her obvious pleasure. And she was not above urging an extra layer of clothing on a guest determined to take a walk in the bracing spring winds off the Hudson River, as John Haines relates in a poem entitled "The Sweater of Vladimir Ussachevsky." Haines, who had homesteaded for years in Alaska and approached Manhattan warily, found the city transformed by Betty's gesture:

> *Facing the wind of the avenues*
> *one spring evening in New York,*
> *I wore under my jacket*
> *a sweater given me by the wife*
> *of a genial Manchurian.*
>
> *The warmth in that sweater changed*
> *the indifferent city block by block . . .*
>
> *It was spring in Siberia or Mongolia,*
> *wherever I happened to be.*
> *Rough but honest voices called to me*
> *out of that solitude:*
> *they told me we are all tired*
> *of this coiling weight,*
> *the oppression of a long winter;*
> *that it was time to renew our life.*

When I first met Betty and her cordial husband, I was much too young to think of "renewing" my life. But in a sense, that is exactly what I needed. After nearly four years of immersion in the otherworldly atmosphere of Bennington, where I had indulged in dreamy self-exploration, gotten high on the studying and writing of poetry, and entered into an affair with a married professor as if it were little more than a rite of passage, I badly needed a dose of practicality. One that the busy Ussachevsky household, artistically charged but also down-to-earth, was eminently suited to provide.

After my nonresident term had ended and I was back at Bennington, I spent most weekends in New York, staying with Betty and Vladimir—affectionately called Dimir. I met my lover on the sly, and would go to readings and museums with Betty if Dimir had other engagements or, as often happened, was out of town lecturing. And I would assist her with any Academy business that she brought home. We planned for my return to New York in September, after my graduation and a summer that would include a cross-country camping trip with my family and a brief vacation in Honolulu. But all that spring, if Betty and Dimir expected to be at their place in Rhode Island, they arranged for me to pick up their keys from a neighbor when I arrived by bus from Bennington on Friday night. I cherished this demonstration of their trust in me, and also the solitude afforded by the gesture. When I had their apartment to myself I pored over Betty's remarkable collection of contemporary poetry and books on icons reflecting Vladimir's upbringing in the Russian Orthodox Church. Their copy of the *London Times Atlas of the World* became my bedside reading; I had never before seen one outside a library. I paced the living room, or sat in a chair for hours, as if I could absorb what it would mean to have a life centered in such a place, a quiet, roomy haven where one could work surrounded by walls full of books, with all the energy and flux of the city just outside the door.

The Ussachevskys' apartment seemed an entire world to me, and even in their absence was suffused with their relationship. For the first time I had come close to a marriage other than that of my parents, and while I knew that both Betty and Dimir would have scoffed at the notion that their relationship was ideal, I felt that they had attained something valuable, a deep and affecting union between two driven and creative people. They had built a marriage that was at once private and welcoming, and I was interested to find, as my parents' marriage had produced four children, that this childless couple, who, as one longtime friend of theirs says, "did not have an easy relationship, but were extraordinarily close," also constituted a family. The best sort of family, in which the members are so at home with one another they create an atmosphere that radiates a nourishing hospitality. I drank it in.

What I took from knowing them was a sense of the balance required for a life in the arts, between living in the practical realm and honoring that which transcends it. Between the freedom and the selfishness needed for creative work, and the discipline required to complete that work in the context of a full life, in which relationships with other people matter. Many of my values come from my parents, whose own intimate yet at times uneasy marriage is now going on sixty-three years. Their parents had marriages of similar longevity. But as a young woman on my own, thousands of miles from my family, I found it easier to learn from Betty and her husband what a marriage means. I took note when Betty remarked one afternoon that she and Dimir had just had a terrible fight. "Was it bad?" I asked, imagining that some earth-shattering revelation would ensue. "One of the worst," she replied. "It was about the little garbage can in the bathroom."

In a sense I became the Ussachevskys' adopted daughter, just young enough to be eager to help Betty paint the barn in Rhode Island, or to spend an entire day protecting trees from a gypsy moth infestation. After Dimir had tilled the garden with his beloved tractor, I would listen to him talk about his father, an officer in the Russian imperial army, who had been the proud owner of the first steam tractor in Hailar, Manchuria. Vladimir had grown up there, in a Russian émigré community, and he described as his first playmates tumbleweeds, dogs, birds, and the wind.

All of this was instructive, both morally and aesthetically, and helped me find a way beyond the impasse I had created for myself in my life and my art. But when the conscience that I had assumed was dead began to wake from its dormancy, I was fortunate to have Betty and Dimir in my life. They had not intended to fulfill such a role, but over time they came to seem like wise grandparents I could trust to judge my behavior with the utmost benevolence, while never neglecting to remind me that I must learn from my mistakes, and not blindly repeat them.

THE HEALTH-GIVING FACULTY

What helped me immeasurably was that Betty Kray never subscribed to the Freudian view that creativity is a kind of illness, an outlet for repressed energies. After my disastrous mescaline trip of 1971, she reminded me that "the imagination is a health-giving faculty," and warned me against toying with drugs that might hinder its

workings. She had recognized in me a garden-variety but neverthe-
less dangerous strain of the manic-depressive cycles she had seen in
other poets. The stories she told me—of finding John Berryman rav-
ing in a hotel room, for example, and phoning for an ambulance as
she picked up from the bed and the floor the scattered pages he had
been working on, drafts of his magnificent *Dream Songs*—were not
simply gossip for Betty.

When I first met her, Betty was particularly sensitive to any self-
destructive tendencies in me, as a poet she had befriended, Grandin
Conover, had recently committed suicide. He was one of many poets who had sought out Betty as a confidante, and she spoke to me
often of his energy, humor, and wit. She had done what she could for
him; when she learned that he was subsisting on peanut butter, she
got him fed, and found him odd jobs of the sort he was seeking, so
that he could pay the rent but also be free to write. And she tried to
get him together with other poets so he would not feel isolated. She
was touched by the letter Conover's parents sent her after his funeral, thanking her for her attentions to their son, and grateful that
Conover's literary friends later had a volume of his verse, *Ten Years*,
published posthumously, with notes by the poet James Scully.

When Betty spoke to me of my moodiness, it was with an air of
exasperation, as if she was impatient for me to move past the adolescent stage of writing only when depressed, which can lead young
writers to create situations in their lives that are likely to make them
depressed, in order to get the poems. The seduction comes in the
promise that art will lift one above petty happenstance and the petty
morality of ordinary people. It might have been predicted that I
would be a sucker for that sort of thing. In my high school yearbook,
amid the cheerleaders quoting Gibran, I chose to put beneath the
senior photo of myself, in the modest sweater and string of pearls

dictated by the school dress code, some misappropriated Kierkegaard: "When a man dares declare, 'I am eternity's free citizen,' necessity cannot imprison him, except in voluntary confinement." By the time I graduated from Bennington, I had misappropriated the Romantics as well, along with the French Symbolists. Artists, I believed, were much too serious to live sane and normal lives. Driven by inexorable forces in an uncaring world, they were destined for an inevitable, sometimes deadly, but always ennobling wrestle with gloom and doom.

Betty Kray convinced me that this was bunk. She counted as friends many writers of the post–World War II generation who had suffered terribly, and often notoriously, from a variety of mental disorders and the self-destructive use of alcohol, poets such as Berryman, Elizabeth Bishop, Robert Lowell, and James Wright. And she was deeply sympathetic: understanding of their pain, and tolerant of their odd and often difficult behavior. But I sensed that Betty saw my naiveté almost as an affront, as though I was confusing the art with the life, and thus committing the grave error of not granting the work of these poets the respect it deserved. Betty was also experienced enough to know that trouble will come on its own, and that there is no fancying it a stimulant to one's creativity. Wanting me to write out of joy as well as despondency, and to dismiss the romance of insanity as a sham, she tried hard to convince me of what her friends who had been institutionalized for madness knew all too well: that sanity, the clean and simple appreciation of ordinary, daily things, is a treasure like none on earth. She was full of sad, sweet stories, such as the one she told about Robert Lowell: Once, as they were rushing to catch a taxicab together, he had tried to relieve her of one of the bags she was carrying. When Betty protested, saying that with a heavy item in each hand, she was well balanced, Lowell bowed and said, "You are very fortunate."

Gradually, Betty helped me stand on even ground. She did not diminish the dangers of life as a poet, especially with regard to the necessity of sometimes shielding myself and my art from the demands of others. But she made me acknowledge that the hypersensitivity to myself I thought I needed as an artist was in fact making me insensitive to other people, and the world around me, and this in turn was short-circuiting my poems. It was up to me to determine what would protect and serve my art, and what would not, and up to me to find others who would nurture me as an artist but also require commitment from me as a friend.

I often felt with Betty that her storytelling about poets, which at times made up a major part of our workday, had a twofold purpose: to incur in me a rigorous professionalism in my work for the Academy; and to demonstrate that my own fears and vulnerabilities were not so bad. While I helped Betty tend to the needs of other poets, I was learning how to take care of myself.

HALF-CRACKED

Caring for poets became Betty Kray's vocation, but her attentions were never condescending, in part because they were both intimate and impersonal. My contemporary Gregory Orr captured the nature of Betty's gift, in admitting that she had always made him feel "cared for," but that "it was not just personal: that it had to do with poetry, which was more important than any of us." Orr had come to New York from Virginia in the late 1970s so that his wife could attend art school. When Betty learned that he was stranded in his apartment with a broken foot, she arranged for him to come to the Academy offices several days a week to screen manuscripts for a competition. Orr says that he read slowly, because the way Betty interrupted him with "wonderful, funny, wicked stories" about poets she had known—Auden, Cummings, Roethke—was so enjoyable. She made him feel that it was all right if a poet was "a little crazy or miserable," and best of all, that "she was including me among the half-cracked poets she cared for."

While Betty was not the sort of person who thought she was put on earth to fix the problems of others, she did what she could to help people cope, often making suggestions that were calculated to make a poet consider embracing change. When A. R. Ammons wrote to her in 1969 that he had hit a rough patch in his life and did not feel up to even a minor public engagement—he had agreed to introduce Richard Wilbur at an Academy reading—Betty responded: "Your letter distressed me beyond words. . . . You are far more important than the little function of acting as an introducer. I wonder if Cornell and Ithaca are good for you? Perhaps you should be in New York where it is hard to live, the congestion is abrasive, and one escapes to the country to gasp clean air and look at clear sky. It's been good for Jim Wright." Wright had by then become a frequent guest of Betty and Vladimir's in Rhode Island.

Not long after I began working at the Academy, a poet took to phoning me daily, fussing—unnecessarily, I thought—over details in the preparation for his reading. When I turned to Betty for help, she told me that I was not to fuss back. She knew the poet well enough to realize that any date set so far in advance would be a magnet for his anxieties, and she gave me useful advice about how best to relieve them. She also related that Louise Bogan, whom she knew I greatly admired, had once phoned her on the morning of a reading to say that she could not possibly appear that evening, as a hurricane was due to strike the city and she could not get her hair done. Betty promised to keep a weather watch, and asked Bogan's permission to make an appointment at a beauty salon, then arranged to have her taken there by cab. She also told Bogan she would be glad to pick her up for the evening reading, an offer that was gratefully accepted.

While Betty might savor the telling of such a story, she never made light of the genuine fear behind it. She knew, as I later learned from reading Bogan's letters and memoirs, that she was an exceptionally brave woman who had faced down much tragedy and internal torment in the course of her life. Betty's goal was to impress on the young people who worked for her that we needed to develop both compassion and professional competence when presenting a poetry reading, and do whatever was necessary to make the event a success. She told us about having to accommodate Robert Frost, in his old age, making certain there were no empty seats visible from his onstage lectern. She would send her assistants to plead with the YMHA staff to fill seats so that Frost would not become angry and fret about imagined conspiracies against him.

Knowing that I was excitable, Betty always checked me out before a reading, to determine whether or not to trust me with a nervous poet. If my voice rose in response to tension, hers would lower. I would feel I had hit a cold spot in the water as she effectively banished me from the Donnell Library's greenroom by sending me on some errand or other. Betty sought to train her staff not to register distress over anything a poet might do or say. Her own calm demeanor in chaotic situations was legendary. Susan Mernit recalls an occasion when a poet who was about to read at Donnell suffered a delusional episode; he thought he was appearing before the Queen

monetary values when one is dealing with a representative of 'culture.'" Three years later, she told Donald Hall: "I am getting fed up with universities filled with English professors who have not heard of poets of your generation [but want only] a big name on a par with a safe reputation. I get furious over how difficult it is to open the doors, and then have to fight for a decent fee."

Betty was matter-of-fact about money, and this allowed her a lightness of tone that complemented her rock-bottom practicality. In 1958, after Robert Mezey inquired if he might receive an advance for his forthcoming reading at the Y, Betty replied, "The accounting department stands pat. The ogre at the pile of gold, even though he's dressed in a Hickey-Freeman suit and a Macy's shirt, remains true. No advances." But, she told him with typical directness,

> *this rule . . . is counterbalanced by the promptness of payment. Checks are made out for the day of the reading. One second after you have read, the check can be in your hand. We have been known to thrust the check into the poet's hand before he begins to read; this is a way of shoring up the nervous ones. Money in the hand steadies the pulse, takes away the tremor, and puts music into a poetry reading.*

Betty's correspondence with poets in her early years at the Y reveals that while she was glad to offer her services, she resisted being taken for granted. "I'm no talent scout," she wrote to James Laughlin, the founder of the New Directions publishing house, who wanted to arrange a meeting between Betty and an unknown poet recently arrived in New York, Denise Levertov. Not wishing to sound altogether discouraging, Betty added confidently, "The small town we inhabit will soon toss us together." The success of her poetry circuits handed Betty another dilemma, because poets began to depend on them financially. Galway Kinnell, who resisted taking a full-time teaching job for many years, has said that the reading fees generated on Betty's circuits helped him stay alive in the 1950s. But Betty had intended the circuits to run autonomously, and thus she could not personally guarantee bookings. She wrote sternly to W. S. Merwin in 1960: "For heaven's sake do not make such statements as, 'I am counting on you for an important piece of next year's income,' a responsibility which I absolutely refuse to accept." She would promise only to "turn up all the engagements I can for you." Likewise she explained to Robert Duncan a few years later that while she would welcome him at the Y, she was not equipped to bring him across the country on the circuits: "I set [them up] deliberately," she wrote, "so as to keep any one person from imposing choices on them."

It is remarkable to me how consistent Betty's solicitude remained for so long, touching the lives even of poets she had not met. She tried for years, for example, to coax the distinguished Brazilian poet João Cabral de Melo Neto to New York for a reading, but could never overcome his doubt that American poets were interested in him. Diane Wakoski first wrote to Betty in 1960, when she was planning to move to New York from California, and the care with which Betty addressed her concerns about the move and the difficulties of becoming established in a new place led Diane, as she later told Betty, to believe that perhaps New York would not be as terrible as she had imagined. A few years later, after they had become friends, Betty commented that she was concerned because she had not heard from Diane in some time. "Whenever letters stop," she wrote, "your voice fades. I worry. Silence in Diane means that warmth has been stifled: what has happened?"

Poets were quick to discern that Betty was not a mere collector of poets, who sought to add "creative" people to her dinner parties for the color and amusement they could provide. Her correspondence is a plenitude of grateful responses from poets, thanking Betty for the care she had lavished on them and their poems. June Jordan, who came to Betty's attention in the late 1960s through workshops Jordan was conducting with disadvantaged children in Brooklyn, and then began sending Betty her poems, wrote to her in 1972 that "everything you say about my work helps me to feel like going on."

Betty once received a handwritten note from Marianne Moore that reads: "I give thanks for these cards, and for you, dear Miss Kray. Stamped! But if you do not specifically realize it, you were commissioned to aid me. . . . I am so inspired by the initiative and the thinking. . . . The simplicity is perfect." Moore's note was in response to a gift Betty had sent her in 1957 when, after her reading at the Y, the poet had confessed that she felt burdened by the demands of correspondents. A box of stamped postcards arrived in the mail, plain but for a blue border and Moore's return address printed in one corner. She used the first of the cards to thank Betty.

THE MIDWIFE

After I left New York, I understood that Betty had given me a standard by which to judge the arts administrators with whom I came into contact as I applied for writing grants or worked in artists-in-schools programs. Having been spoiled by Betty, who, as Diane Wakoski said, had diligently championed poets and poetry "with no self-serving interests whatsoever," I was ill equipped to deal with closeted poets who had settled for administrative posts but were still angling for recognition of their own work and resented the artists in their employ.

I became increasingly aware of the value of Betty's clarity about where she stood, her refusal to manipulate the writers who advised the Academy or judged its prize competitions, for the simple reason that they were poets, and she was not. For all the expertise she had gained, Betty never presumed to judge what poets needed. "In all of our work together," Stanley Kunitz commented, "I can't remember her ever saying that poets 'should' do this or that." Betty's consideration of poets as fully adult persons contrasted sharply with the way others often regarded writers as gifted but terrible children, wonderfully creative but much too irresponsible to be trusted with the details. I was once invited to join a group of artists in offering suggestions to improve a program that we had worked in for years. The woman we were speaking to nodded cheerfully at everything we said, and took not a single note. She was baby-sitting us while the real work was being done elsewhere, by accountants, consultants, and the development staff. Betty would have fired the lot.

No small part of Betty Kray's legacy is the training she gave to a new generation of arts administrators. Gigi Bradford is one of those who apprenticed under Betty's expert tutelage, going from the Academy to a position as poetry coordinator at the Folger Shakespeare Library in Washington, D.C., and later becoming director of literature programs at the National Endowment for the Arts at a critical time in its history, when its very existence was being threatened, and fellowships for individual artists were being eliminated by conservatives in Congress. Bradford says that Betty's methods of making a friend here, a friend there, at whatever institution she was working with, and thus building a reliable group of allies, had helped her save the Endowment's writing grants, the only such fellowships that survived the hostile climate of the mid-1990s.

Rachel Bellow, who had been recommended for her Poets House job by her MacArthur Foundation colleague Gerald Freund, and who later went to the Mellon Foundation, said, "I learned from her the pressure of being the midwife, and not the mother. Betty took obvious pleasure in recognizing her proper role at a birth. It never occurred to her that she was an arts administrator. She knew her strengths, and no one ever pigeonholed her into being merely the logistics person." Most important, in Bellow's words, "Betty knew that she wasn't the artist, but she wasn't a bureaucrat either. She came from another era. With Betty, arts administration was not a profession, but a passion." But by the 1980s Betty sensed that passion was no longer enough. "I now hear dogmas pronounced to me that come from experimental practices that I initiated but that have hardened into procedures that little resemble the original," she noted. "The stridency of tone suits the hard-edged professionals. I was an amateur."

THE READER

Betty would have gladly admitted to being an amateur when it came to appreciating poetry, but at least she read it. I was dismayed to realize that many arts administrators, although they pride themselves on being promoters of "culture," feel it beneath them to actually read the work. By contrast, Betty had a delicious way of letting poets know their work had been keenly appreciated, so that even in a cramped airplane cabin their poems might come alive. In 1962, Betty wrote to the elderly Katherine Garrison Chapin that she had taken Chapin's most recent book on a plane trip. "I like to read during the limbo of passage. I grab at words to make a counter-tension to take-off. So in this condition and in flight myself I discover all kinds of motion stirring in your poems. It was wonderful to be occupied with the planet turning; time and objects moving; light, birds, animals, water, all in motion; and perception itself making a kind of flight. My airplane tinkered along in contrast."

Many poets valued Betty's responses to their work not because of any specific advice that she offered, but because of the perceptive encouragement she provided even when a poem was in its early stages. Galway Kinnell remembers having sent her a rough version of "The River," and says that "while Betty knew that the rudimentary thing I'd sent wasn't the thing, she liked the endeavor, what I was trying to do . . . so I kept sending her different versions of it." David Ignatow too was inspired by Betty's interest in his work: "She had an empathy for writers that I have rarely seen. . . . She drew me out and I wrote like mad, because I felt I had someone behind me."

In my experience, Betty had an uncanny way of knowing when a poem was not yet working as it should. In the early 1980s, I showed her a draft of a poem that I sensed would be important to me as a catalyst for new work. My instinct was correct, as the poem did release my creative energies after a dry spell, and soon I was dealing with a cornucopia of poems, and my first essay on the subject of religion. But Betty's initial response to this poem was to make objections that were specific enough to let me know I still had work to do.

Betty later recalled to me that the poem, entitled "The Blue Light," was "not doing its job. Obviously," she remarked, "it had a significance for you that it was not conveying to me. You were in an excited state and I hesitated to make any big criticism. I remember that I quibbled a little." What she thought of as a quibble, however, had been exactly what I needed, as she had pinpointed the spot where I had begun to go off track. I am by no means the only poet who came to consider Betty the best reader I ever had, one who would press on with hard but useful criticism, if she thought it would help me do my work. She was above all honest. Of a revised but still-not-there version of "The Blue Light" that I had sent her, she wrote:

> *You can't rely on a few commonplace words—angel, blue light—to give the reader the experience you are trying to convey. There must be an angle, a wrenching, a terror someplace . . . like 'Tiger, Tiger,' or Christopher Smart. I believe him. I don't believe you. (I do hope you understand what I am saying here, else it will sound like a barrage of insult.) What I am trying to say is that to describe simple, pure, intense experience requires a drowning of self in the oblivion of language. There can be no self-consciousness. Then the experience comes out of a language that is personal, convincing, and yet absolute.*

Her words nearly overran the paper she was typing on, and the letter, signed "love from Betty," sent me back to brood over the poem, which I had set aside for months. Betty's challenge jarred me into making major changes, and I replaced some of the abstract words that had troubled her with images of human beings. The poem, which is about my experience of nearly dying in a hospital as an infant, now contains the nurse who, my mother told me, had fed me a bottle throughout my operation, and a doctor whom I describe as "working helplessly, with all his skill." Thus peopled, the poem was better able to stand on its own.

I always sensed that Betty's faith in my work centered on the fact that I so eagerly embraced the process of revision. Soon after I met her she said that she liked to see my early drafts because I knew what to do with the comments she made. Thus it was that Betty became the primary reader of my poems-in-progress. And she kept abreast of my editing of the manuscript for my first book. When it was time to submit a final version to Paul Carroll and Pat Meehan, my editor at Big Table, Betty and I met at the Harbin Inn restaurant on Broadway, a place where we knew we could work undisturbed for hours. We received deferential treatment there because Betty's husband often ate in the restaurant kitchen with the staff, conversing in the dialect of the province of Manchuria where he had grown up.

Betty and I fiddled leisurely with the order of the book. Occasionally I would read a revision aloud to see if the new version passed muster. I think of that evening as a watershed because it became clearer than ever to me that the imagination works not so much through inspiration as through perseverance. One must slog through the false starts, spot the wrong words and hold out for the right ones, and above all, be vigilant about staying on the path of revision, no matter how uncomfortable or even painful the journey might become.

Betty and I worked hard that night and we also celebrated. I wanted to dedicate the book to her, but she advised me not to use her name. We agreed to a compromise, a dedication "To the seaweed harvester," referring to the times we would stand in the surf at Moonstone Beach and grab large, waxy strands of seaweed for her garden compost. Betty announced that she intended to give me a publication party at her apartment. She warned me not to make too much of the book, though, and over the next few months loaded me with stories about the dangers of early success, which she regarded as a curse, particularly in literary New York. "People will pick you up," she said, "because they collect artists as if they were butterflies. You become a thing of the moment, all too easily discarded." In her view, John Malcolm Brinnin, who had preceded her as director of the YHMA Poetry Center, and Jean Garrigue, who had edited an anthology of verse for the first of Betty's translation projects, had both suffered from being lionized in their youth. She felt that they had never quite gotten over being praised as poetry's golden boy and girl, and as their careers faded, they had become bitter.

As it happened, my little book was born, lived, and died without having much impact. Published in October 1971, *Falling Off* went out of print not long after, never having earned out the advance of $500, which had been my prize money. But the book's impact on me personally was momentous, and when Betty read the signs of my postpublication blues, she talked me into applying for a one-month residency at the Fine Arts Center in Provincetown, Massachusetts. Soon after I arrived there, I sent Betty a letter detailing the adventures of my long bus trip from New York. And I wrote of one day that began with a solitary walk at dawn along the seashore and ended with my baby-sitting the young daughters of another artist. I enclosed samples of a few not very successful attempts to write in my new surroundings. Betty replied that "the drama and shock of change may be important for the writing of poetry. . . . The beginning is isolation, and eventually a penetration into community life. This, I had anticipated, but baking cookies with energetic little girls I had not." Betty encouraged me to keep working on the poems, which I sensed were not very good. She did not disagree, but insisted that there was something of value in them, that in "the in-between places, the cracks . . . I hear counterpoint." Betty's use of a musical metaphor underscored for me the strength of her conviction that I should keep trying.

Under Betty's tutelage I realized that by believing too strongly in my own "creativity," I had left myself vulnerable to the fear that the well could run dry, that the next poem would never come. This is a common fear among young poets, and it can take years to dispel. Even mature writers develop anxieties about the time it takes to write poems, and grow frustrated over hours, days, and weeks that seem lost to distraction. To not be writing, and writing well, can be depressing. But the largeness of Betty's faith in poetry sustained many poets through difficult times, and words she wrote to Jane Cooper might serve as balm for anyone grown weary with the fits and starts of the writing process. In response to a note Cooper had sent, along with drafts of work that would be included in her book *Maps and Windows*, published in 1974, Betty was forcefully re-assuring:

> *You say you weren't writing in Maine, but visiting, walking— well, you were accumulating your poems, germinating them. . . . They will be wonderful poems when they come out, never fear their slowness. I've been ordering perennials for a border, and these seeds when they come must get nipped by frost, frozen; one puts delphinium seeds, for example, into the freezing compart- ment, to freeze them into ice cubes. In cold November one plants the ice cubes, and this stimulates them to hurry a little bit; otherwise they are frightfully slow.*

Yet Betty was not an easy reader to have, as she often probed a poet's primary concerns. Her conversation, even in social settings, tended toward serious matters. You might mention, in passing, a childhood experience, and Betty would ask a question that would trouble you all night. In the morning you would begin the poem about the experience that you had always meant to write. Although I don't know of anyone who had the nerve to call Betty a muse to her face, there were many who found that her amiable curiosity had helped them face a topic that had seemed too large, too deep, or too painful, and had remained dormant until Betty stirred the waters. In the early 1960s she received a sheaf of poems from Louis Simpson, accompanied by a brief handwritten note thanking her for having asked him to write about Jamaica, his childhood home. He was to set many poems there, as well as a prose memoir. Jane Cooper credits Betty with keeping her at work on an essay entitled "The Children's Ward," which relates Cooper's experience of being hospitalized as a child. "Betty could be reproving," according to Cooper, "and had a long memory. When I would send a new version, Betty would critique it in light of the old, saying, 'You changed the end, and it's not as good.'" She encouraged Cooper for years: "Betty's urgings brought me to the version I have," Cooper says. "She chided me, and she made me write."

Betty had known the poet Mark Strand in New York, but became much closer to him after he took a position at the University of Utah when her husband was teaching there. In May 1987, after being told that her cancer was terminal, she wrote to Strand, "I've got the summer," and then got down to the business at hand, a group of poems he had sent. "Whatever it is, the studio up in the air . . . a certain isolation—it has done something astonishing to your poems. Not that you were ever a slouch, but these seem to have leaped into a language absolutely vital to them." The poems, later published in Strand's book *The Continuous Life*, attracted Betty because they were not depressing, even though they dealt with "grim inevitabilities. It is quite a feat," she told him, "that they can concern the terrors of the human situation without hand-wringing."

At the time she wrote to Strand, Betty was facing the inevitability of her death from cancer and was undergoing radiation to provide a measure of symptomatic relief. She was extremely reticent about herself, so much so that what she resented most about her illness was that it made people fuss over her. Rather than elaborate on her pain, which, when pressed, she characterized as "discomfort," Betty would light up with talk about a fellow patient on the cancer ward, a lonely widower who had taken a fancy to her, or an Irish nurse whose voice, with "a lilt right out of the Book of Kells," Betty had found soothing when the woman tended to her late at night.

The nurses at the Harkness Pavilion of Columbia-Presbyterian, a ward for cancer patients, frequently had to question Betty about her symptoms. But she would sometimes turn the tables. She once said to a favorite nurse, enticingly, "You know, I've been thinking about you, and I think I know how I'd describe you to someone who had never seen you. But there's one thing I couldn't tell them: Are you a Democrat, or a Republican?" The woman laughed and said, "Well, if inheritance means anything, my father was a Democratic mayor in a little town upstate." And Betty, also laughing, replied, "I knew you had some Democratic blood!" As the nurse talked on about her father, Betty relaxed; she had won a skirmish in the battle to take the spotlight off herself.

During one of my last visits with her, Betty said that she'd been thinking about a metaphor she had first employed at our long-ago dinner at the Harbin Inn, which by 1987 had vanished, as is the habit of many a favorite Manhattan restaurant. That night Betty had compared the process of revising a poem to that of a snake shedding its skin. She said she was impressed at how I would emerge from a period of sluggishness and despair with work very different from what I had written before. "The poems come out clean and shiny," she had said, "as if free of the former faults, and in a new voice."

I was startled to hear Betty bring up the image again, and told her that I had not forgotten it. I had seized onto it, like a lifeline, and for years, whenever my thinking grew clouded and dull, and writing seemed completely dead in me, I would remember Betty's metaphor, and tell myself to wait. I would dare to hope that her conviction would hold true, that powerful but unseen forces were at work that would eventually find release in new writing. When I began to read the Bible as an adult, I recognized in a Gospel parable a version of Betty's faith in the processes by which poems come to be: "The kingdom of God is as if someone would scatter seed on the ground, and would sleep and rise night and day, and the seed would sprout and grow, he does not know how." Betty's belief that writers must always be willing to submit to processes of change that are unknown to them is akin to what the Benedictine tradition regards as the never-ending process of conversion that keeps faith alive. The trick is to maintain stability and change in balance, so that one remains grounded and yet avoids a narrowing of scope.

Another contradiction that Betty embraced in her work with poets is that while the art must stand on its own, the life itself is not entirely separate, but as the wellspring of the poetry must be as carefully tended, and as open to revision, as any poem. She believed that people needed relationships that forced them to look outside themselves and connect with others, and thought that one of the best vehicles for this was to settle into what she termed "the rock-bottom stability of marriage." Shortly before my wedding, she wrote me: "If we were trees we'd have rings of more intense color to show for the effects of marriage."

Betty once sent me a letter that bristled with concern over a friend's pattern of engaging in affairs with his students, which had approached a manic intensity. He had turned to Betty because his poetry was stagnating, and she told him, soberly, that "to move through a profound change in his marital relationship"—her polite way of telling him to stop having affairs, or get out of the marriage—"would . . . help him make an equally profound move in his creative life, with the effect of deepening and producing new kinds of poetry."

I have no idea what this man made of her remarks, but I saw in them Betty's faith that people have it within themselves to undergo profound and necessary change. I wrote to her, after I had moved to South Dakota but before I felt truly a part of it, that at first I could not write, and then I could not help writing. When I sent Betty drafts of the first poems to come out of inhabiting my grandparents' house, she responded with a resounding Amen: "Change simply expresses the fact that one has been able to discover some new power in oneself. It was there all the time, but it needed a trail hacked open to find it."

Chapter

Ten

TONASKET

THAT THE PATH I CHOSE FOR MYSELF WAS in the South Dakota town where my mother had grown up astonished Betty as well as my parents. Not one of them thought I would stay more than a year. And as it became clear that my husband and I were indeed settling in on the Plains, I found myself having to defend my choice to remain: No, I was not "wasting my education"; yes, I could remain connected to the larger world; no, I would not sink into a Chekhovian funk, no longer able to live in the city but immobilized by nostalgia in the country.

When I tapped into a hitherto unsuspected vein of domesticity, learning to knit, and to bake bread in my grandmother's kitchen—her built-in flour bin and kneading board were irresistible—my mother and Betty expressed surprise and concern. After a casserole recipe I entered in a competition at the county fair became a semi-finalist, and I participated in a bake-off, the two of them conferred over the phone, and Betty suggested that an invitation to New York might be in order. As my husband's first book of poems, *Ariana Olisvos,* had recently been published by the University of Massachusetts Press as the winner of the Juniper Prize, she thought that he might read on the Academy series. We drove to New York in my grandparents' ancient Oldsmobile V-8 and stayed with friends in the city.

Betty respected the impulse that had led me to seek a new voice in old territory, and recognized that by moving to my grandparents' house I had placed myself in a rich environment for the gestation of poetry. I wrote to her frequently, trying to convey my feeling that the old house was listening to us, wrapping itself around us as if it were now responsible for the lives and secrets of four people, the couple who had built it and inhabited it for more than fifty years, and the newcomers, who wore the trappings of domestic intimacy but had put off marrying. For a time David and I allowed our neighbors to assume that we were husband and wife, and when I told Betty that their curiosity had tempted us to invent a wedding date, she warned, "Truth-telling may be vague and contradictory; lying must be precise," and duly described the way people often responded to her meandering style of speech: "For this reason I am always believed when I lie, and deeply suspected when I tell the truth."

I began attending my grandmother's Presbyterian church, and told Betty I had discovered that I loved hearing Scripture read aloud. She replied that I reminded her of Bill Merwin, who had returned to his parents' house after their death. His father had been a Presbyterian pastor, and Betty detected in the poems Merwin had written there a new sense of theological language. I hadn't noticed anything of the sort cropping up in my work, but my love of the Protestant hymns had sent me back to reading Emily Dickinson. "Those old hymns are still worth everything," I told Betty, and in response she sent me a copy of Dickinson's *Selected Letters* for my birthday.

My everyday life felt richer than in New York, if only because my social milieu had expanded from people mainly my own age to include four generations. In a single day I might converse not only with a neighbor's small children but with their great-grandparents. I began attending baptisms, weddings, and funerals on a regular basis; by contrast, in New York I had not witnessed a single one. I wrote to Betty about the children who, when I began working at the town's public library, would come in with insects in jars and ask my help in identifying them, and about the generation of elderly friends I had apparently inherited along with the house. My grandmother had noted the seventy-fifth birthday of a neighbor on the kitchen calendar, so I took a bouquet of flowers—my grandmother's columbines, which had survived my ineptitude as a gardener—to help her celebrate the day. I was not prepared for the emotional reaction I received. My grandmother had been her best friend, the woman tearfully explained, and after she died she did not expect that many people would remember her birthday. And I described to Betty a Sunday dinner for which David and I arranged to spring a ninety-five-year-old former sheep rancher from the nursing home. My husband had promised to cook her anything she liked, and she requested pan-fried chicken with mashed potatoes and gravy. She told us stories about using a coal-fired stove when she was a young woman on the ranch, and of riding horseback for many miles, her good shoes in a saddlebag, to attend Saturday-night barn dances.

With a sly and girlish grin, she asked our permission to dip the homemade bread into her gravy.

This environment soon drew forth a group of poems. The first were about going through my grandmother's things and, although I could not articulate this at the time, my sense that I had moved to South Dakota because of her, wanting to change my life and my work but not knowing how except to place myself in her home. Years later I found a similar experience related by Larry Woiwode, who in his essay "The Spirit of Place" describes beginning to write seriously in New York in the mid-1960s; he adopted what he terms a "modishly experimental" style "on the cusp of postmodernism," influenced by such writers as Beckett, Kafka, and Nabokov. But one day, he recounts, "my maternal grandmother entered my mind with such force it occurred to me that she had influenced me more than any of these writers." The revelation led him to write about his grandmother in what may be the ultimate North Dakota novel, *Beyond the Bedroom Wall*. Woiwode now lives and farms about fifty miles north of me.

In 1974, I could not foresee where my new life was going, but I kept sending Betty the poems as they came, telling her, "I always seem to write to you when bread is rising." The period of waiting for dough to rise was conducive to the writing of both poems and letters. Betty answered that she liked the direction my work was taking, and I credited this to the widening focus I experienced in a place where I no longer felt pressured to compete with other poets. I now lived among people who neither knew nor cared about the vicissitudes of literary business (except, memorably, when I happened to tell the Presbyterian pastor that after years of trying, I had finally sold a poem to *The New Yorker*, and he announced it the next Sunday morning, amid news of births and weddings, as one of the "joys of the church").

I settled happily among neighbors who were ranchers, truck drivers, tavern owners, contractors, and merchants, and in their presence, my poems, like my life, could not help becoming less cerebral. There were odd moments, but they made for good stories. When an older couple invited us to dinner—he was a banker of my grandfather's generation—the sight of my tall, husky, bearded husband entering their home prompted a neighbor to phone to ask if they were all right, or if he should telephone the police.

I learned to appreciate the moments when my old life touched the new, as when an issue of *The Nation* arrived in the mail, containing a poem I had written in New York and a profile of South Dakota's maverick senator, James Abourezk. I wrote poems about the landscape that surrounded me, and sent them to magazines. Betty mentioned that Gregory Orr had recently confessed that while much of my early work had left him cold, he would accept the poems I had recently submitted to him at *Virginia Quarterly Review*. "How much she's changed," he told Betty, and she gladly concurred. The poems that I was slowly accumulating became another book of poetry, published ten years after my first. The titles alone reveal the difference: I had gone from *Falling Off* to *The Middle of the World*.

But Betty's worry that I might become too isolated on the Plains never left her, and over one winter, when my husband and I were without a car, I felt she might be right. In a long letter written during a solitary weekend she had spent in the city, she said that "one needs the long winters, the enforced self-confrontation, but the minute it starts acting like a prison, then you have to change something, maybe just—just!—yourself." Striking one of her constant themes, she added, "It has always seemed to me that writers need community." Betty approved of the steps David and I had taken to establish local literary connections, by attending annual conferences with other writers in the Black Hills and becoming poets-in-the-schools for the South Dakota arts council. My husband had bravely confronted his terror of small children and his dislike of proselytizing for poetry by joining me in the classroom, and we were both amused when a fourth-grader in Mobridge listed our visit as third in the great events of his school year. The first was a visit by a basketball star from the Lakers, a local boy made good, and the second a stern lecture about crime given by prisoners on tour from the state penitentiary. Two poets had been icing on the cake.

Since Betty saw reading as a way to commune with other writers, living and dead, soon after my move to South Dakota she started sending books she hoped would provide some context to my rural life. The first was Edwin Muir's lovely autobiography chronicling his childhood in the Orkney Islands. Then came several classics on village societies, Ronald Blythe's *Akenfield*, and Ann Cornelisen's *Torregreca*, which set me to thinking about the western Dakotas as the Calabria of North America. Later she lent me Wole Soyinka's affecting memoir of his Nigerian village, *Ake: The Years of Childhood*, and a book (whose title I have forgotten) that I loved for its description of matriarchs in a French village who gathered at a communal bread oven to discuss how the day's humidity would affect their dough. As I told Betty, one plumber, who was described as moving perpetually among several jobs he had begun and then temporarily abandoned, had a counterpart in my own town. These books impressed on me the sense that any human habitation on the face of the earth might give rise to its storytellers, and planted in me the seed of an idea that I might one day write a prose book about the remote part of the country where my grandparents had settled, and my parents grew up, and I had chosen to return.

Betty also sent me Elizabeth Gaskell's *North and South*, which inspired my first essay on the subject of the Dakotas. I could see the conflict that Gaskell described, between the people of England's sophisticated and cultured south, and those of the more rough-hewn north, echoed in tensions between America's East and West, and also in the Dakotas themselves, where the population increasingly resides in burgeoning cities along the states' eastern borders, while small towns in the west languish.

Betty had found Mrs. Gaskell in her exploration of late-nineteenth-century and early-twentieth-century literature, which started in earnest when she read *Howards End*. "There is some kind of key here that has become my obsession to find," she wrote me. Perhaps it was all very simple, she said, and "the key is ourselves. I think my question began with wonderment over how I became middle-class and urban." I was not to understand the full import of Betty's words until well after her death, but at the time I gladly accepted the books she sent as tools for survival in a new environment.

Betty, I understood, was trying to ease her own mind. While she felt that my move to South Dakota might be necessary for me as a writer, she could not let go her fear that I might stagnate in so remote a place. "You're isolating yourself too much from other writers," she would write reprovingly, "you need to get out more." Because I did not have the funds for travel, Betty sent me copies of current literary magazines, and furnished me with the names of new poets whose books I might purchase by mail or obtain through the state library. When an aspiring poet wrote to Betty from a ranch in eastern Oregon, saying that she felt isolated from other writers, Betty suggested that she write to me, and we corresponded for a time.

Betty was delighted to hear that a friend and I had driven two hundred miles to Aberdeen, South Dakota, to attend a poetry reading by William Stafford. I had last seen him when he dropped in at the Academy during a visit to New York, and he had indulged his love of photography by snapping shots of us in the office. When I approached him after the reading, Stafford grinned and said, "Betty told me you were out here. I've had you on my radar."

What I was not to know for many years was that as a young woman Betty Kray had longed in vain for someone to put her on the radar, and to connect her to a world outside the rural area in which she lived. Or that the town in South Dakota where I had moved was, in its physical isolation, social demographics, and agriculturally based economy, a place very much like it. All of Betty's years in New York, during which she became a fixture in the city's cultural institutions, could not diminish the power of Tonasket.

TONASKET

In the supermarket—how much of a New Yorker am I? I press against the supermarket's dairy bin and the refrigerated air wells up over me out of the past, the dark, cold air of the apple shed in Tonasket. My feet are ice cold and my sinuses begin to ache. The checkout cashier, a Puerto Rican girl with a scarred mouth and a pleasant face, packs my grocery bag and winces when she lifts a heavy bag of onions. What hurts? The pain bites into my right shoulder. It's from lifting over and over with the

same arm. I'm feeling old. Yes, I say, at nineteen, I felt this
pain. I'm getting old, I thought, and I haven't even gone to
college.

These words, written in Betty's familiar scrawl, fill the center of a paper plate that I found among her papers after her death. The word "Tonasket" was familiar, but since Betty so rarely talked about her past, it took me a moment to recall that Tonasket was the small town in Washington where she had gone to high school, and then worked at odd jobs—packing apples and hauling them by truck to Seattle—until she had saved enough money to enter the University of Washington. Betty's sensitivity to women's fashion had stemmed from that period, when she could not afford the stylish sweater sets worn by Seattle girls, and defiantly trooped around in what was then uncommon attire for women, blue jeans and flannel shirts.

Betty met her husband in 1943 while working for the head of the university's Far Eastern studies program; she'd become intrigued with the young man who had looked over her shoulder one day as she perused a map of China. He pointed out details, such as a misplaced railroad line, that were incorrect, and told her he had been born into a Russian community in Manchuria. In the late 1920s, when Vladimir Ussachevsky was in his teens, his father, an army officer, was arrested during civil unrest and deported to the Soviet Union. After the family learned that he had been executed, an older brother who had immigrated to the United States managed to get his mother out of China. In 1930, Vladimir joined them in California, and eventually he obtained a degree in music at Pomona College. He was in Seattle on wartime duty as a translator for the army. He and Betty shared a love of music and literature, and they married in February 1944. Later that year they moved to Washington, D.C., where Vladimir was a research analyst on the Far East for the U.S. Army and the State Department, and Betty developed cultural exchange programs for the Institute of International Education. In 1947, when Vladimir was appointed to a post at Columbia University's music department, they moved to New York, and Betty found work with an organization providing services to refugees displaced by the war in Europe. In the early 1950s she and a friend founded Craymore Associates, an agency that helped composers and poets with the logistics of lecture and reading tours.

Like Betty, I had come as a young woman from the West to try New York City on for size. To become a New Yorker—worldly, cultured, urbane—seemed a good and desirable thing, and Betty was an inspiration. By the time I met her she was a true denizen of the city. But, as those words she had scribbled on returning from the grocery store made clear, Tonasket loomed.

Tonasket, Washington, is a remote village of a thousand people in the Okanogan Valley, 250 miles northeast of Seattle by two-lane highway. It was a place Betty Kray felt lucky to have escaped, a sour memory jostled to the surface by the pained face of a young checkout clerk in Manhattan. Many veteran New Yorkers come from such towns, and over the years they invent a convincingly stylish urban self. But Tonasket remains lodged in the memory, the fear of being trapped in the cold storage room of an apple orchard. Nineteen years old, and no way out.

Betty seldom spoke of Tonasket to me when I lived in New York, but after I left for South Dakota, she would summon her experience there to help me understand what I was witnessing. When I wrote to her in the early 1980s, at the start of America's perpetual "farm crisis," to tell her that many pastors and teachers in my area were coping with "secret" meetings and anonymous hate mail designed to force them to leave, she responded, "I am accustomed to these situations. I grew up among them in Washington state, which accounts for much of my suspicion and hostility toward small-town people. My favorite English teacher was practically drummed out of town because she had us read Huxley's *Brave New World.* (My mother and father fought for her.)"

Betty regarded the enforced insularity of rural life with a wary eye: "We settle down in our burrows and become more and more ingrown, habit-ridden den animals. We like only those who share our smell. Strangers come and upset us the moment we get a whiff of them and their difference." Like many young people who feel stifled in small towns, Betty had found it easier to live among a mass of people and was relieved by the anonymity of urban life. Yet she also understood that a small town "ultimately can turn out to be as tolerant as the city. . . . Acceptance may come about, but it's a slow process. It means that you've become part of the landscape, like a weathered post, and they'll put up with you." She did accept that David and I were indeed settling in; I loved my part-time work at the public library, and David was elected to the city council for two terms. Amused, Betty credited this to all the upstate New York Irish politicians in his ancestry. But she never lost her uneasiness about where we had landed, and never came to visit, even though she and Vladimir sometimes drove between Utah and New York.

Betty's attitude toward life in the rural West might be summed up in her reaction to a gift from my husband. He had sent her one of his favorite novels, Marilynne Robinson's *Housekeeping,* set in a small town in Idaho. It tells the story of two children's pitiful attempts to make sense of the grown-ups around them, who in their smugness are blindly and gratuitously cruel. Betty confessed to us that the fictional town had reminded her all too keenly of the place where she had been a teenager, and that she had felt compelled to skip to the end of the novel. "I had to make sure," she said, "that someone got out of there alive."

GETTING OUT ALIVE

Betty Kray lived very much in the present, effectively discouraging speculation about her past. But her story in many ways epitomizes the journey of the American immigrant into the mainstream. Her mother was from a Pennsylvania Dutch family that had come to America in the 1600s and settled in southern Missouri. Betty was taken with their heritage and history, but was cool to her father's side of the family. I did not learn until after Betty's death that her paternal grandparents had homesteaded in the Sand Hills region of Nebraska, a few hundred miles from my home in South Dakota. In the nearly twenty years that I knew Betty, I never suspected that her family history was so familiar to me, a classic tale of both failure and tenacious survival on the Great Plains.

Betty's paternal grandfather was a tailor from Prague named Krajieck who had immigrated to America with his wife late in the nineteenth century because he sensed that war was inevitable, and he did not wish to serve in the military of the Austro-Hungarian Empire. Like many European immigrants, the Krajiecks were seduced by the promise of arable land on the Plains, and in Nebraska they built a sod house surrounded by a vastness of land and sky. The family grew to include ten children. The tailor found that he was not suited for dry-land farming on an isolated homestead, and after years of coping with crop failures caused by droughts, grasshopper infestations, incessant wind, and prairie fires, he abandoned the family. The story is a common one: on the western Plains, some eighty percent of homesteaders left within the first ten years and returned to cities in the East, glad to trade the heroic independence of the farmer for the security of a steady wage. Often it was a tough woman like Betty's grandmother who remained on the land, working it with her children.

Most Great Plains children from this era received very little in the way of formal education. It was usual, until after World War II, for families to regard a high school diploma as a luxury. At ten or twelve years of age, boys would leave school to work for their parents on the farm, and girls would become domestic laborers in small towns or cities, providing their families with desperately needed cash. Willa Cather's *My Antonia* chronicles the deprivations of the early generation of Great Plains homesteaders, and also the tensions between native-born Americans and Czech or Bohemian immigrants. The Krajiecks, unlike many immigrant families, always had books in the home, and a high ambition fueled by the memory of European culture. Betty's grandmother faced severe economic hardship and social opprobrium in ensuring that each of her ten children completed high school. Betty's brother, who related the family history to me, said that their father used to speak of "gruesomely hard times."

As the oldest child, Betty's father, Richard, had borne much of the responsibility for the family after their father left. One sister, Elsie, went on to marry the first sheriff of Wyoming, Dewey Riddle, and the couple maintained a large ranch near Yellowstone Park. Betty's father attended the University of Nebraska, where he received a degree in civil engineering. A specialist in hydraulics, he found work in Denver and married, and his first child, a son, was born there in 1911. Richard worked in the Everglades for a French firm that went out of business at the start of World War I, and then found a job in Cleveland, where Betty was born in 1917. In the 1920s, he changed his last name, simplifying it to Kray. The family remained in Cleveland until the 1930s, when the Depression put Richard out of work again.

The Krays moved to the home of Betty's maternal grandparents in Tonasket, where Richard became the town's engineer and surveyor, and Betty's mother, Gertrude, assisted her recently widowed father, William Mohler. He was a member of the River Brethren, a Pennsylvania Dutch sect that had moved west in the early years of the twentieth century, and when the Krays arrived in Tonasket he was well established as a nurseryman and a lay pastor in his church. Betty regarded the move as an unmitigated disaster. Having attended a well-equipped and relatively sophisticated high school in Shaker Heights, Ohio, she resented her new school and town, where resources were limited and new ideas were suspect. She also rebelled against the strictures of the River Brethren. In a rare personal revelation, she once told me that although the church believed in breaking the will of a child, it had never gotten her. Her recalcitrance had been a burden for her mother, and Betty regretted having been a difficult daughter. But she had felt it necessary for her survival.

THE MUTE WORLD

Betty's experience of the River Brethren left her with a lifelong distaste for the didactic use of language. And it did not take much to stir the embers into flame: I remember the intensity with which she criticized a poet when she felt that he had used the occasion of his

Academy reading to preach to the choir a mix of leftist politics and environmentalism. Although she agreed with the sense of what he had said, Betty regarded his heavy-handed style as a betrayal of the art of poetry, and of language itself.

A junior high school administrator in Brooklyn once thanked Betty for sending Paul Blackburn into his school to shock his students out of what he called a language vacuum. He felt that Blackburn's reading of his own poems in English and translations from the Spanish had given the students a sense of the dignity of their everyday speech. Because Blackburn was a man who lived by the word, his very presence had helped students who had been starving for a language of their own.

I was surprised by the avid manner in which Betty seized on this idea of language in a vacuum, making it a focal point for her desire to bring together poets, teachers, and schoolchildren. With my relatively sheltered middle-class life—my parents, as musicians and teachers, always had books and music on hand, and encouraged articulate discussion around the dinner table—it was a revelation that one might have to leave home in order to find a language. But in New York, I was surrounded by people who had done just that, Betty Kray among them. A simple request from Denise Levertov, asking if she might dedicate a book of poems to her, elicited a revealing response: "If you put me on your dedication page," Betty wrote,

> *I should want to be Betty Kray. As such I couldn't be called an "ardent and steadfast friend of poetry," which maybe Elizabeth Ussachevsky could smilingly and publicly accept, but Betty Kray, my childhood name, is closest to my real self, and as BK I scarcely befriended poetry but rather used it ruthlessly ever af-*

ter discovering it. I think poetry is to be used. It's like an otter's toboggan slide, it's for fun, merry-making, a quick plunge, of infinite use. I'm trying to figure out how to explain to you who grew up in an atmosphere charged with language how it was to have grown up in a relatively mute world, as I did. Or at least where language was regarded as a practical instrument for everyday dealings or as a didactic instrument, and as such blunt and heavy, a killer.

The best language I heard spoken I now realize was that of my mother, whose speech came from a small southerly town where the style was simple and vividly related to the physical landscape. A refinement of college and gentility overlay this speech, but as she grew older the refinement dissolved into the understratum. My grandfather wrote didactic articles and as a consequence spoke pompously, but would lapse into a biblical idiom—he was a Bible reader—and this saved him. My father tried to sound like a cross between an engineer's and a lawyer's brief, a composite of the two. They (and the community) were essentially non-fluent.

Betty explained to Levertov, "If one is not used to hearing original ideas, and feelings, articulated by ordinary people, then language becomes a nagging puzzle." And in the 1970s, as she approached the age of sixty, she was still attempting to decipher the puzzle of her "non-fluent" past. She wrote to me:

I now realize that I grew up swathed in the American myths that came out of dime novels. "A lady greets her laundress with the same courtesy she would extend a duchess," said my mother, and this always impressed me; I thought it was original, but

now I recognize it as an echo from one of those novels. "We are
as good as anybody else on earth," my father would say fiercely.

The fluency of poetry had taken Betty past platitudes, immersing
her in a secret spring, hidden and forceful. "Poetry takes one to the
fountain," she wrote. "It's a main stream, a river Jordan sluicing the
barren west."

Poetry had offered Betty a way out of Tonasket, but she knew
that there were "barren wests" everywhere, and she developed an
instinct for smelling out the beast of provincialism. After a 1963 trip
to Kansas City to promote her poetry circuits, she told Robert Bly
that returning to New York had been a relief. With insightful exacti-
tude, she reported that in the city, while "the bitterness, meanness,
selfishness of people is active . . . at least it works in an exposed
vein. What curdles me is that these things are disguised as something else in provincial people; one wants them straight without any
gloss of morality or moral justification. Better to hear somebody
snarl, 'I want my way,' than, 'I am right, you are wrong.'"

Betty believed in the sanctity of place, and the necessity of
putting down roots. But she also knew that a legitimate pride in the
uniqueness of one's region can easily become a smug and suffocating force that attempts to exclude all outside influence. After several
months with Vladimir in Utah, she longed for New York. "The trouble with Utah," she wrote me, "is the complacency of its population,
thinking it lives in the best place in the world, the most beautiful,
and also thinking that it is self-sufficient. That is why it's provincial."

As someone who is a partisan of both New York City and a rural place where the words "New York" are generally said with a sneer,
I find Betty's comment prescient and useful. She takes me beyond
regional divides, into the heart of the matter. Whether we live in

Manhattan, New York, or Manhattan, Kansas, it is self-satisfaction that dulls us, and the belief in our self-sufficiency that is the killer. We grow resistant to change and thus are more likely to project onto outsiders our deep-seated fear of the other.

I saw a vivid example of this during my tenure at the Academy when Betty hired a young poet, Miguel Ortiz, to work in a junior high school on the Upper West Side of Manhattan. He read poems in an English class, and initiated an after-school poetry workshop that he enhanced with an exploration of the new technology of video-tape, teaching students to film one another reading their poems and to record their impressions of the city. There were few Hispanics on the school's faculty, and Ortiz became tremendously popular with students, many of whom were first- or second-generation immigrants from the Caribbean and Latin America.

The Academy received word from the school principal, however, that an older teacher had complained because Ortiz was reading poems containing obscene language. When Betty investigated, she discovered that the words in question were everyday Spanish phrases, images of vegetables in a grocery store bin and of mothers carrying infants. Stunned, Betty engaged the protesting teacher in conversation. He eventually revealed that he had always wanted to be a rabbi but had more or less settled for teaching in a public school. What gave him the most pleasure in life was attending classes after work at Yeshiva University.

We had stumbled onto an urban tragedy in microcosm. As long as his school and neighborhood had remained predominantly Jewish, this man felt at home in a self-contained world. But the recent influx of immigrants left him feeling under siege, and he equated Spanish words with everything vile. By giving legitimacy to the native language of his students, the poet had become the focus of his resentment. I had not yet heard Betty speak of Tonasket, Washington, but now know that in this sad and frightened man she had encountered its ghosts. He had never dared to enlarge his perspective, and the failing had deprived his students of an education that was rightfully theirs. He had cut himself off from them, and from a literature that might have helped him make essential connections to his community. Instead, he had bitterly set about to turn an ordinary junior high in Manhattan into his own xenophobic backwater. Betty defeated him by threatening to drown him, and the school principal, in literary paperwork. She proposed to the principal that both men read in advance every poem that Ortiz planned to present to the students. As Betty had expected, this offer was rejected, and Ortiz was able to continue his work.

Betty was pleased that so long after she had dreamed up a means of getting poets together with schoolchildren, I was earning the bulk of my income from its offspring. The artists-in-residence programs in North and South Dakota schools for which I worked for more than a decade were administered by state arts councils that had not existed when Betty originally approached the New York City Board of Education. She loved the stories I sent her from isolated hamlets too small to have a hotel, tales of boarding for weeks in people's homes—"You're like a nineteenth-century schoolteacher," she commented—and working in one- and two-room rural schoolhouses with children who wrote about rattlesnakes and the smell of new-mown hay.

Betty died before I could relate an episode that would have resonated deeply with her. On a snowy afternoon a teacher's aide approached me in a school library, asking if I could help one of her charges. She pointed to a glum-looking teenage girl seated at a table across the room and said, "She has to come up with three metaphors for English class, and she can't think of any." Introduced to the girl as "the visiting writer," I found that my mind was empty, and all I could do was sputter phrases that clearly made no sense to her. "But you make up metaphors all the time," I finally said, "and you have since you were a child. It's how you learned to talk . . . it's how the English language works, how your mind works, not something you have to learn about in school." The girl gazed at me, blankly, miserably, and I realized that if, as Czeslaw Milosz has said, language is the only homeland, this girl was an exile in her own country. And I had been placed before her, then and there, to do what little I could. I made up simple comparisons that I thought might register, and penetrate her dense silence. "Have you ever said that someone's heart is ice, or a newborn baby's face is a wrinkled apple?" I asked. The girl, still mute, worked up a smile and stirred in the uncomfortable plastic seat. She gave me a desperate look and said softly, "My father is a dandelion."

Her expression told me that she was expecting me to ridicule this assertion, or to shoot it down by grading it with a D. Instead, genuinely fascinated, I said, "Now, that's original. It sounds like poetry to me. Can you tell me more about the metaphor, just why your father is a dandelion?" The girl explained that when he was in a good mood he was bright and sunny, but when he lost his temper he was like a dandelion gone to seed, blowing his anger all over the place. I told her I loved the metaphor, because everyone knows that those tiny seeds, like anger, take root and are almost impossible to kill. "It's a metaphor that anyone can understand," I said, "but it's also yours, because you are the one who discovered it." The girl glanced at me as if she suspected that I might be putting her on, but she also looked relieved, even proud. The moment passed, and I thought of Paul Blackburn's students in Brooklyn and of Betty in

Tonasket. She might have whispered to the girl: *Get out—get as far away from this place as you can—while you're still young—get out of the barren stream before it dries you to a husk.*

E R A S U R E

If in her youth Betty Kray had felt constrained by language that was tuned to argument and utilitarian purpose rather than to beauty, she spent the rest of her life making up for it. She had grabbed hold of poetry and then used it, as she once said, as "a form of self-charity." And she never stopped helping others to use it as well. Even in the last year of her life, Betty had her ear to the ground, working on a grant proposal for Poets House to provide backing for writers among New York immigrant groups: Filipino poets writing in English, Spanish, and Tagalog; French-speaking poets from Quebec, Haiti, and Martinique; and a group in Queens who called themselves by a Quechua word Ollantay.

Betty had used New York to draw a world of poets to herself. And the world came. It was fitting that the poet she had worked against great odds to bring to America in the mid-1960s appeared, unexpectedly, at the memorial service that Betty's friends held a few months after her death. Andrei Voznesensky happened to be in New York in April 1988, and he came to the church and waited patiently until other poets had spoken. He knew that it had been extremely difficult to bring a Russian writer to the United States at that time, and he expressed his gratitude for Betty's persistence and for all that his subsequent contacts with her and with American poets had brought him.

Listening to Voznesensky and the other writers that day, I

tried to imagine what Betty would have made of it all. She had always been resolute to keep the focus off herself and give poets center stage. Stanley Kunitz described her essence when he said that
Betty

> *was disinclined to talk about herself, even in her last illness, but*
> *once she told me that . . . there was an ancestor who had settled*
> *in Nebraska during the trek westward. Something in her open*
> *countenance and singularly measured speech reminded me of*
> *that prairie heritage. She kept a level, blue-eyed gaze on the lit-*
> *erary scene, ruefully aware of its follies. About the power that*
> *she wielded she was disarmingly diffident, preferring to think of*
> *herself as a laborer in the vineyard.*

Betty became acutely aware, however, that her habit of remaining in
the background and designing programs to be taken over by other
institutions had often meant that she did not receive credit for her
ground-breaking work. In more than thirty years of working on behalf of poets, she was awarded only one public honor, a citation from
the Mabel Dodge Foundation that came in the last year of her life.
And less than a year after her death, Betty's name was omitted from
a 1988 *New York Times* article celebrating the YMHA Poetry Center's
fiftieth anniversary. This erasure grieved Betty's widower anew, and
baffled me until I contacted one of the sources for the article, the
elderly John Malcolm Brinnin, and heard him angrily deny that
Betty had ever been the Center's executive director. He was so in-
tractable that I didn't have the heart to tell him I had found in
Betty's papers much evidence, including YMHA brochures from the
period, that contradicted his assertion.

Likewise, Betty's name appears nowhere in a 1986 article on

the origins of the poets-in-schools program by Leonard Randolph, a former head of the literature program at the National Endowment for the Arts. He speaks only of "a very small pilot program funded through the Academy of American Poets, which was placing writers in schools in a half-dozen major cities." His tone suggests that the idea of getting poets into classrooms originated at the NEA, when Betty had been working on her grant proposals even before the NEA had come into being. In the early 1970s the NEA did appropriate and expand the Academy's program into all fifty states, and included not only poetry but painting, sculpture, dance, and drama as well. But Betty's name was lost in the process, and with it the sense of all that she had done, in the words of Harvey Shapiro, to "thread labyrinthine bureaucracies so that our voices could be heard." In the twelve years that I worked in the Dakotas with teachers enamored of Kenneth Koch's books on teaching poetry to children—*Wishes, Lies and Dreams* and *Rose, Where Did You Get That Red?* —which had come out of his workshops with students, sponsored for years by Teachers & Writers Collaborative, I found no one who knew that it was Betty Kray who originally persuaded the reluctant poet to work with elementary students instead of teenagers, and the Academy that had sent him to Manhattan Public School 61 in the spring of 1968.

When he heard that I was writing about Betty, Gerald Freund told me he was glad, because he was tired of dealing with young arts administrators in the nineties who proudly announced as innovations programs for writers that strongly resembled the poetry circuits Betty had created in the fifties, or the community-based library programs she developed in the seventies. "They have never heard of her," he said, "and give me blank looks when I tell them that from my perspective, they are reinventing the wheel." Versions of programs that Betty had dreamed of but which never got off the ground—

ing to interfere with the poets who judged Academy competitions, worked well enough when trouble followed a Lamont selection, as when William Harmon's lively *Treasury Holiday* brought complaints about what some Academy patrons perceived as obscene language and unpatriotic sentiment. The policy proved less effective, however, against the cronyism that accompanied the increased professionalism of poetry in the 1970s and 1980s, when poets frequently rewarded colleagues, former MFA classmates, or their own students with fellowships and prizes. Student poets sometimes selected an academic program in writing on the basis of how much pull they thought the faculty had with arts institutions, and the members of self-perpetuating boards such as the Academy chancellors often chose new members who were like them: white male college professors. Both Betty and the Academy had difficulty adjusting to the changing times, and the thorny issue of inclusiveness was one that Betty was never able to resolve. She had wanted the Academy to act as the nation's clearing house for information about poets and poetry, but in the 1970s had to yield to Galen Williams's newer, more flexible and populist institution, Poets & Writers, whose newsletter quickly grew into a major resource for American authors.

In order to appreciate the accomplishment of Marie Bullock and Betty Kray, one must envision what was available to American poets in 1934, when Marie Bullock began talking nonsense about funding an annual fellowship, or in 1954, when Betty Kray dared suggest that colleges in a region band together to sponsor young poets to the tune of $100 per reading, or a decade later, when she came up with the harebrained idea of having poets visit school classrooms to talk about poetry. The two women indelibly changed the landscape for poetry in America.

The Ignominy of the Living

"The ignominy of the living!" Betty exclaimed, more angry than I had ever seen her. She was on her way out the door of our sublet in Yorkville. David and I had invited her for dinner, and she had walked home with me from work. David was out buying fresh fish and vegetables, and I had put an early Bob Dylan record on the turntable because Betty said that while she had heard me speak highly of him, she had never heard him sing. Her reaction was something neither she nor I was prepared for. Overcome with a disdain that left her muttering incoherently about a young man she had once known who had also written and sung songs of protest, she recovered only enough to say, "I need time by myself—I'll just walk over to Gracie Park and back."

I needed to catch my breath as well. Something about the Dylan recording—his raspy voice, the political nature of the songs—had summoned for Betty the ghost of the young man who had been the first love of her life. In the late 1930s he left Seattle to join the Abraham Lincoln Brigade, and he had died in the Spanish Civil War. His memory had surfaced with such force that Betty had become angry all over again, struck bitter by the brutal death, and a new generation's famed singer who seemed to Betty a pale imitation of her unremembered friend. "The ignominy of the living," she repeated, shaking her head as she went out the door. When she returned a half-hour later, she was her familiar self again, and did not want to discuss the matter.

The intensity of Betty's reaction reminded me of an experience I'd had with her in May 1969, when I had traveled from Bennington to spend a long weekend in her apartment. A phone call came from someone, who, when I said that I did not expect the Ussachevskys to be back from Rhode Island until late that night, left a simple message: "Please tell them that Marion died." When I passed the news on to Betty, she sighed, gazed into my blank face, and said, "Of course, you wouldn't know." As I helped her with the bags that Dimir was hauling in from their car, she added, "I mean, you don't know the context, but to suddenly be told that you've lost someone who used to be very important in your life, a long time ago, is very strange." And she told me the first of many stories about E. E. and Marion Cummings, whom she had gotten to know in 1954, when the poet hired Betty as his agent for readings. She and Dimir lived in the Village then, not far from the Cummingses' Patchin Place apartment, and Betty became a regular visitor, going every Friday afternoon for tea. She was then a vivacious woman in her late thirties, Cummings was sixty, and his wife, Marion, a former model, was forty-eight, and keenly aware that Cummings had divorced his second wife, a woman closer to his own age, in order to marry her.

Long before Betty arrived at their doorstep, Marion Cummings had adopted the role of Cummings's protector, and she remained cool toward Betty, especially when Betty and Cummings developed a daily ritual, so that

> *every night around ten o'clock he would come by, tap on my window and I would go with him on a long prowl through the Village streets. We walked and I listened and he talked about himself, about the world, about the things he loved. I disagreed with much of his political belief but held my tongue; he was quite vulnerable during this period. . . . He would disprove over and over again the critics' charge that neither his poems nor his paintings showed "development"; this to him was the most in-*

tolerable of all the criticism. What I liked best was to have him
reminisce about his early years in New York, and he told some
fine stories.

Betty said that many things she and Cummings witnessed on these
nighttime walks later appeared in his poetry. She particularly de-
tested a maudlin verse about a little Christmas tree that they had
glimpsed in a tenement window, and groaned when I said I had
found it done up as a children's book. And while she once commented that she had found Marion Cummings somewhat frivolous
and enamored of her own beauty, she admired her steely resistance
to the petitions of would-be biographers after Cummings's death.
"Marion reports that [they] keep her angry," Betty wrote to a friend,
"which in turn keeps her in good health. She is busy saying 'no.'"

Now that I am in my early fifties, around the age Betty was
when I met her, I have grown all too familiar with the experience
that she found so disorienting, the sudden loss of someone who, in
passing away, takes part of your own life as well, erasing a bit of what
has made you who you are. And young people are dazzling in their
inability to comprehend the momentous nature of what has occurred.

Betty Kray was an intensely private person, who shared only
pieces of her story with many different friends. No one person, except perhaps her husband, had the complete picture. It is not likely
that she told anyone whether or not she had an affair with Cummings. He may have pursued her, yet a personal observation about
him to me—that he had seemed determined to remain twenty-six
forever—might indicate she had the good sense to resist. And I
doubt that Betty often told the painful story of the man she had
loved when she was barely twenty, who died fighting fascists in

Spain. But her cutting remark about how ridiculous we living are, as we bustle along with little sense of the deprivation we suffer in our ignorance of the past, has stayed with me. When I read Saint Benedict's admonition in his Rule for monks, to "day by day remind yourself that you are going to die," I think of Betty's face contorted by a freshly remembered grief, still potent after more than thirty years. I find that the saint, and Betty, continue to give me perspective on matters of life and death.

After my husband was diagnosed with cancer several years ago, in my mind I heard Betty's diffident tone as she shrugged off her own diagnosis: "Everyone has to deal with cancer these days." And as I gradually adopted the role of my husband's caregiver, I thought of her insight into how others so often used her, her warning that "it is hard always to be 'strong.' And if one is cast in that role for too long, the illusion of one's strength becomes more and more tenuous, a trap. I begin thinking that I am hollow and a fraud." Whenever I feel hollow and weary, I think of Betty's steadfast loyalty to her friends. A professor of neurochemistry who had been the Ussachevskys' neighbor in Manhattan for many years told me that when her husband was dying of a brain tumor, suffering both physical incapacity and an unpleasant personality change that caused many of their friends to stop visiting, Betty demonstrated a profound understanding of his deficiencies, and came over every day to help care for him and to give the woman emotional support.

James Wright's death, in 1980, was a turning point for Betty, reminding her of her own mortality and inspiring her finally to step down as the Academy's executive director. She planned to help Dimir write about his family in Manchuria, Russia, and America, and began gathering information from the Ussachevsky relatives who had settled in California. She also hoped to write up her poetry walks as a compact literary history of New York. In a letter to Galway Kinnell, she said that the devastation of Wright's cancer had made her feel that she had "lost the man I knew," and in words that recall for me Wright's own poem "A Rainbow on Garda," with its image of "Christ, frightened and dying / In the air, one wing broken, dying, all alone," Betty described feeling "involved as a spectator in the manner of death, all the more meaningful because it was the suffering of someone I had known, but who had become as abstract and simultaneously present in his dying as Jesus."

Betty Kray understood death and dying. Her mother had succumbed to cancer, and Betty explained to me that it was during her illness that she realized how terrible it can be when the world seems to be passing you by. The sense of being forgotten begins when people lose touch with you, both figuratively—they stop phoning and writing—and literally, as they grow afraid to come near. The poet Cynthia Macdonald thanked Betty for telling her how significant touch can be to a dying person. Betty's advice had led Macdonald to hold her mother's hand as she lay in a hospital bed. "I saw immediately how important that was to her," she wrote Betty, "although she might never have been able to ask for it."

Betty did not seem to fear death as much as being forgotten. Her many friends knew she was undergoing chemotherapy, and did not wish to intrude, but the lack of mail and phone calls made Betty feel isolated. Her husband, Annie Wright, and I contacted poets around the country who had been dear to her, asking them to call or write. Stanley Kunitz sent a snapshot of his garden in Provincetown at the height of summer, a photo that Betty treasured. Tomas Tranströmer sent a thoughtful letter; Galway Kinnell wrote a note and phoned. Betty's friends were relieved to hear that she could tolerate brief visits at home, and it revived her spirits when young poets came by. Amy Bartlett brought her infant son and a gift of colorful turbans to help Betty disguise her hair loss. Henri Cole and Nancy Schoenberger, who were then working at the Academy, brought in a Chinese meal and picnicked with Betty in her living room.

In the fall of 1987, I returned to New York when Betty was due for another round of chemotherapy. Dimir wanted me to conduct formal interviews with her, and I would time them around the treatments, trying to catch her before the drugs made her feel, as she once put it, as if she'd been hit by a truck. I would take the bus up Broadway to Columbia-Presbyterian, and report to Betty on what I had observed along the way. She was eager to hear about life in the city; an account of a toddler holding on to his grandfather's hand as the two navigated a busy sidewalk would make her smile.

During this time I stayed with Dimir in their apartment, and almost felt that we were desecrating Betty's kitchen by cooking microwave dinners there. When it was time for her to leave the hospital, I helped Betty into the panty hose she insisted on wearing for the brief trip home. I had not realized before how difficult even small things become when one is seriously ill. While Betty resented her unaccustomed helplessness, she was not too proud to ask for help. A few days later I went to a Russian Orthodox church to light candles for Dimir and Betty, and stayed for the two-hour liturgy. The music eased my anguish, and seemed to suspend time itself. When the service was over, the congregation was invited to partake from a basket of antidoron bread—it has been blessed but not consecrated. I had never seen this type of bread before, each piece consisting of two white knobs of dough. "It is for healing," an old woman said, in response to the question on my face. She nodded when I asked if I might take an extra one for a friend. But Betty was asleep, and Vladimir and I ended up eating it in the kitchen, both of us in tears.

I was at home in South Dakota when Betty's heart gave out during her admission to the hospital for a final round of chemotherapy. She had been scheduled to enter a hospice in a week, and she dreaded the move. Rachel Bellow phoned me with the news, relieving me greatly by telling me that when she had last seen Betty, propped up by pillows on her living room sofa, she had seemed more at peace than ever before. Rachel said, "She was like a warrior who had set down her weapons and let her arms drop to her sides, completely at rest."

she taught me. Our kitchen is watched over by a hand-carved totem of a polar bear that Vladimir picked up for Betty on a visit to Alaska. He gave it to me after her death, and I keep it perched on a high shelf.

When I spread the immense piles of paperwork spawned by my husband's illness on our kitchen table, trying to reconcile medical bills with insurance statements, I recall how outraged Betty became when she found that the name on the letters from Blue Cross was a fiction, a mere signature stamp. And I picture Annie Wright, who came to help when Betty and Dimir were not able to keep up with the barrage of bills, resolved to straighten out the mess. It helps to know that, even in this, I am following in the footsteps of Betty and her friends.

I remember Betty when I regard my childlessness, because she taught me how to be a childless woman who pays close attention to children and their needs. I remember the perfection of her gesture, when we were near the Central Park Children's Zoo and she saw a boy who looked lost and about to cry. Betty knelt down and politely asked if she might lift him so that he could spot his mother in the crowd. He nodded, and a tearful reunion ensued. On another occasion, when Betty and I were on the Broadway subway heading uptown, we stood next to a girl at the front of the crowded train. The child was torn between enjoying her view of the lights in the tunnels as we sped along, and stealing nervous glances back at her parents, who were seated in the car. She said aloud, to herself, that she must be sure to get off at 116th Street. And Betty replied, in a reassuring tone, "We're getting off there too." The girl looked up at us, nodded, relaxed, and became happily absorbed again in the lights and the motion of the train. It is a small thing hardly worth recalling, and yet I do, the grace of knowing just the right thing to say to another.

I find a contradictory Betty present on my bookshelves, in the battered old *AIA Guide to New York City* that she gave me after she had used it in researching her literary walks, and in a well-worn paperback, an early edition of Edward Abbey's *Desert Solitaire*, that she had urged on me many years before. Next to it I find more of Betty's loves, the Scottish writer Gavin Maxwell's *Ring of Bright Water*, which she cherished for its descriptions of otters, and *King Solomon's Ring* by Konrad Lorenz, with its close, affectionate observations of swans and greylag geese. Betty lent me the book in Rhode Island after we had gone to an Audubon preserve near Moonstone Beach to watch swans teaching their young to fly.

And I think of Betty whenever I look at the books of my poetry that Ed Colker has lovingly made over the years, accompanied by his prints. He was a regular at Academy readings in the 1960s, attending so often that Betty grew curious. Upon approaching him, she found an artist who devoted much of his time to printing and illustrating the work of contemporary poets, notably Michael Anania. I was fortunate that Betty invited me to have lunch one day with her and Colker, as he expressed an interest in my poetry that I was not accustomed to at the time, and our own friendship took hold. In the ten years between my first and second books of poetry, Ed provided me with a much-needed affirmation by printing a limited letterpress edition of the work I was writing in South Dakota.

Betty still advises me in literary matters, and it is when I am struggling with the blank page that I feel most at one with her. I laugh, seeing an apt description of myself in a comment she made after struggling to compose a report for a foundation:

> *I never have any idea of what I will say until I start. It's a deplorable mental condition, of which I am sure most people are*

not guilty. I wish I were the sort who could sit down with an outline clearly in mind and unreel the items from my brain to the typewriter; but no, I must waste hours on the report and then throw out almost the entire draft, having found what I was to say, finally, in the last paragraph.

Betty was the first teacher I had who could not conceive of teaching except by example. It is not the easiest way to learn. Through her I came to appreciate that the fuzzy way my own mind works—I too have never been able to compose from an outline—was the tool I had been given, and it was enough. When I turned to Betty to help me improve the prose of an Academy letter, or revise a poem, I would encounter, in the words of Gerald Freund, "a great conspirator." But like many great mentors, Betty did not think of herself as a teacher. At the retirement party given for her by the Academy in 1983 she was uncharacteristically flustered by the praise heaped on her by several generations of poets. After they had spoken, and C. K. Williams had presented her with a book of handwritten verse that he'd gathered from poets across the country, Betty stood and addressed us in a voice ragged with emotion, but also a hint of exasperation: "Don't you understand? For all these years, you have been my teachers, and this is my graduation party!"

From Betty I learned that a true vocation becomes such a part of you that you never stop living it. Larry Joseph, a young poet Betty had befriended near the end of her life, told me about a reading that he gave with Louis Simpson in May 1987, which she had come to. It was the last she attended. Joseph noticed Betty staring intently as he read, and later realized that this was her way of dealing with pain: to focus on something that mattered more. Afterward she cornered him to praise his reading style, and to offer advice that sounded very much like what she had told me when she helped me prepare for my first major reading, in 1970. She made me practice, with a tape recorder, before a tolerant audience of the Academy staff. "Just trust the poem," she said, "and let it lead you."

Betty believed that writing poetry could lead you through all the vicissitudes of life, but only if you learned to shed the vanity of self-consciousness and allowed the poem to speak for itself. She understood that writing is an endeavor that is born in solitude but that ultimately embraces a host of other people. Many poets who benefited from her attentions would recognize themselves in June Jordan's recollection that "when Betty Kray befriended my poetry and me, I was quite a young poet," unused to giving readings or knowing what to make of her poetry in a broader context. But, Jordan reflects, "through the inspired intercessions of Betty Kray, I moved into a public maturity." And she found that Betty's "faith, not only in particular poets, but in American poetry, deeply affected my own sense of the national and international possibilities for our solitary art."

When I am tempted to diminish the possibilities inherent in the art of writing, and shrink my world to the size of a toothache, allowing a perceived slight or unfairness to fester into resentment, I hear Betty commenting that for another poet, a friend of ours, "bitterness had become a permanent substratum." Betty coolly assessed a prodigiously ambitious poet who had obtained a position that he'd coveted, the directorship of a prominent writing program: "It won't satisfy him; before long it won't seem enough. It is never enough." I am grateful to Betty for pointing out that the desire for power can become an end in itself. And I am glad that when I first tasted the bittersweet fruits of success in Manhattan's poetry world, I had a mentor such as Betty to remind me to watch what I wished for. She set a high standard against which I still measure myself, as I try to keep in mind that gratitude, not complaint, is in order if I am to pull myself out of the undercurrent of narcissism that feeds most professional jealousy.

I am grateful too for a magnificent gift I never asked for, the necklace of large turquoise pieces strung on a rough cord that Betty impulsively hung around my neck one day. While it looked odd with the old T-shirt I had worn to sort through her papers in the hot, dusty upstairs of the Rhode Island house during her final summer, I knew it was a momentous gesture, and somehow correct. For many years, whenever Vladimir's work took him to a place, such as New Mexico, that Betty had wanted to visit, he would bring her back an offering of semiprecious stones. Strands of amber from Russia, or carnelian from Brazil. The shock of seeing me wear the turquoise pained Vladimir, but there was no going back.

As Betty had taught me how to live, she also allowed me to see what it is to die, and to let go, not just of the beautiful gifts accumulated over a lifetime, but of the failures and loose ends that might torment one's final thoughts. She stopped complaining that the irreplaceable documents and photographs from Vladimir's family that she had hoped to turn into a book had been lost in the mail. And while she still regretted not doing the things she might have done had she left the Academy sooner—writing a memoir of the poets she had known, planting more trees in Rhode Island, completing a text to accompany photographs she had taken of her rural neighbors there, or obtaining more financial support for a group she had recently founded, the Claremont Walking Society, whose exclusive function would be to promote literary walking tours in New York City—she seized on the time she had left and took pleasure in what little she could do.

Betty began truly to inhabit a world she had once described to Diane Wakoski after observing a woman feeding cats in Morningside Park, in the shadow of St. John the Divine. "I could sit in a circle of cats," she wrote, "just as I can put a circle of people around a table with food, and feel as if I have performed one of the best functions in life. . . . But periodically I turn against the cooking, the washing, the tending that it demands, and turn to nature. Then I feel that the wind, the rock, the trees, and the meadow are company enough." Once she had finally given up "tending," and allowed herself to be tended to, all that Betty had loved about the country and the city intensified for her. The scent of rosemary through an open window, or sheets just in from the clothesline near her garden, people walking dogs and babies beneath a canopy of autumn leaves in Riverside Park, the glint of the Hudson just beyond.

I keep a map of the New York City subway system on a wall in my house in South Dakota, to tell me where I've been, and to remind myself of a marvelous irony in my friendship with Betty: that we met over a map of the United States in her office, and that although she might have told me then, or at any time in the years I knew her, that she also had roots on the western Plains, she never did. I also try to keep in mind the healthy balance she maintained, between valuing what she termed the "wide-lens landscape of the West" and New York City, "with its incredible, compressed human lives." I can't enter Manhattan without thinking of her, and recall that when I would visit from South Dakota, our usual lunch would be something we could take to a bench in Central Park, near the Academy offices. A pretzel from a vendor, a piece of fruit, a container of yogurt from a deli. But before the eating and the gossiping, Betty would slip off her shoes and raise her face to bask in the greenery and sunlight.

"WE SHOULD FORM A COMPANY"

In a letter to Jane Cooper from Rhode Island, Betty counted as members of her community

> *a neighbor's dog who considers himself part of the family, by which I mean, he tears up our compost heap, chases our rabbits and woodchucks, sleeps on my bed of lily-of-the-valley, and takes dog-naps outside our door, panting so that you can hear him all over the house . . . [and] the hawks who nest in the woods in back of the barn and circle the fields, the mockingbird in the little Norway maple, the flycatchers who raise a family in the old apple tree, the hornets who think the front door is theirs and contest our right of way. We sit at table gossiping about them all: "The mocker's been imitating the whippoorwill again. The swallows really did chase the hawks away. Have you recently seen the bull snake by the compost heap?"*

Betty told Cooper that she dreamed of finding a way to provide poets of modest means with a place of refuge such as she and Vladimir had established for themselves in Rhode Island by purchasing acreage in the 1950s, when the land was cheap. It was one of her regrets that she had not arranged to turn it over to a foundation to be preserved as an artists' retreat, and as it happened, Vladimir became mortally ill not long after Betty's death and never managed to get it done. But Betty hoped, as she told Cooper, that writers might "own land in different places communally . . . some . . . in Rhode Island, some in Maine, some in Utah," and band together to fight for taxation according to land use, preserving "the tilth, the beauty, the forest of the land," and resist being taxed at the real estate value, which, she said, "penalizes everyone but real estate developers. I think we should form a Company."

In retrospect, it might be said that "forming a Company" was Betty's response to everything. She did it informally, by habitually gathering a brood of poets, young and old, whoever wanted to come, after readings at the Donnell Library. Hundreds of American poets recall what Carol Muske has characterized as "being herded" across midtown Manhattan into Hell's Kitchen, to the Greek restaurant Molfetas, "to eat, drink, and schmooze." Soon after he arrived in America in 1972, the exiled Russian poet Joseph Brodsky became a regular at Academy readings, having found that they helped him become better acquainted with American poetry, while the long, intense discussions at Molfetas afterward allowed him to get to know American poets.

The official "company" that Betty Kray formed in the last few years of her life, Poets House, now honors her with an annual poetry walk across the Brooklyn Bridge, and the Elizabeth Kray Award (informally known as "the Betty"), which since 1998 has been given biennially for "service to the field of poetry." Although the very idea of "the Betty" makes me glad, I sense that Betty herself would object, asserting that it was not she who had served poets, but the other way around. She would be more pleased to learn the extent to which, according to Margo Viscusi, president of Poets House, her ideas have been kept alive through its programming: the "Passwords" series, in which one poet discusses the influence of another; collaboration with other institutions, including city parks, libraries, and schools; an award for the teaching of poetry, given in conjunction with the city's annual high school poets' competition; the sending of poets to discuss literature in branch libraries, part of a constant effort to bring writers to reading their great heritage, a living community whose voices reach back beyond Homer; the biannual People's Poetry Festival, a stew of oral, experimental, and performance poetries; and a newly established endowment for an annual translation event. All of this, Viscusi comments, can be traced to Betty's enthusiasm and initiative.

"I PRAISE AND GLORIFY YOUR GREAT PATIENCE"

In the early 1980s, when I was experiencing the first, thrilling wave of a religious conversion, Betty commented that "playing around with elation can be dangerous." She wrote to me: "Oh, I know this mood of Kathy's. She's discovered herself well, full of energy, and the world interesting, and she is blazing at the glory of it all." I knew that Betty was warning me not to allow my manic mood to slide into depression.

For the first time in my life, I told her, poems were coming out whole, as if they had formed in my unconscious before speeding through my hand to the paper. But Betty had heard it all before, and recalled other poets she had known, John Berryman and Anne Sexton, for whom religion had fed creativity but also fueled manic behavior in unhealthy ways. She did not count my new high as "religious experience, which is not ego-centric. But it seems the kind of thing that would make you feel exposed and vulnerable." She was on full alert.

"My advice," she wrote, "is to stop putting yourself in these new and interesting contexts . . . just so that you [will take] the focus off of self. I like the thought of poems coming effortlessly, but also the counter-balancing thought of going over them in quiet, in effect in meditation." She hoped that this discipline would help me find a way of using my manic moods creatively, while keeping them subordinate. Once again, Betty became my most difficult and most rewarding reader. While she did not find in my new poems the didactic tone she had feared might intrude, it was hard for her "to find your poems expressing what I believe it is you are feeling. This discrepancy interests me very much, and is, I think, one of the most important challenges you've ever run up against." On reading this I felt that Betty, like a good spiritual director, had opened my eyes to the problem I was facing but had not yet been able to articulate for myself.

Betty urged me to turn outward and read: "Go back to the visionary poets. Try Wordsworth . . . try St. John of the Cross—not my dish; I tried years ago and failed. Have you read Tolstoi's homilies? Read about [St. Teresa] and her accounts of ecstasy. Read Whitman." And she referred me to the medieval tale of a juggler who gives the only gift he can give to the church, juggling before a statue of the Virgin Mary. "It is the same point," she wrote, "that Tolstoi makes in his tale of Martin the Cobbler, to serve by doing what one does best. Martin cobbled shoes. You write poetry. Whatever you are feeling or undergoing, your poetry should be able to encompass and embody. If it can't, then you must stretch, pull, alter, until it does."

When I was working on my book *Dakota*, I sometimes felt that Betty was looking over my shoulder, hoping to find something to help her comprehend her ancestors' travails in western Nebraska. And as I unraveled the tale of my own religious heritage, in *The Cloister Walk* and *Amazing Grace*, Betty was listening closely to make sure that my language remained alive, and did not grow stale with preachiness. On an index card that I installed near my desk, I copied

Betty's scathing but eminently useful observation on my first, fevered attempt to write an essay about the influence of religion in my life: "You are in danger of making proper little genuflections to scholarship, when what you need is the poet's voice."

A poem, after all, renders an experience that is more than mere opinion, idea, or doctrine. And it is as experience that a poem stands or falls, inviting the reader not to debate or argue but to respond with both heart and mind. An essay too, as Cynthia Ozick has written, "is a thing of the imagination. If there is information in an essay, it is by-the-by. . . . [It] is the movement of a free mind at play, [and] closer in kind to poetry than to any other form. Like a poem, a genuine essay is made of language and character and mood and temperament and pluck and chance."

When it comes to the way that my own character has unfolded over the years, Betty might agree with me that in my typical topsy-turvy fashion—a trait I share with her—I have effectively reversed the scenario set forth by Wordsworth: "We Poets in our youth begin in gladness; / But thereof come in the end despondency and madness." When I first met Betty, I leaned on despondency like a crutch and flirted with madness. I tend more to gladness now, and Betty has much to do with that. But it is also God's handiwork, God's insistence on being active in my life even when I am unaware of it. I am reminded of my New York days every time I sing the words of Robert Robinson's eighteenth-century hymn "Come, Thou Fount of Every Blessing": "Jesus sought me when a stranger / Wandering from the fold of God." Although I would have rejected this notion at the time, I now believe that God was there all along, present even in seeming absent. In whatever ungodly circumstance I thoughtlessly placed myself, God was there, a silent watcher and infinitely patient companion, waiting for me to come to my senses.

When I encountered this passage by the thirteenth-century mystic Saint Gertrude, it brought my own youthful follies to mind. "I praise and glorify your great patience," Gertrude writes,

> *which bore with me even though from my . . . childhood, adolescence, and early womanhood, until I was nearly twenty-six, I was always so blindly irresponsible. Looking back I see that but for your protecting hand I would have been quite without conscience in thought, word, or deed. But you came to my aid . . . and provided me with necessary correction from those among whom I lived.*

"Correction" is not too strong a word for what I needed then, as my blithe irresponsibility had blinded me to the fact that others were as real and as vulnerable as I. The mistakes of youth may be necessary, even as a means of correction, but it is grace that provided me with a company of schoolmates, coworkers, poets, friends, lovers, and strangers who endured, chastised, and blessed me through some difficult years, helping convert a girl nicknamed "The Virgin of Bennington" into a woman who is more at ease within herself, and also more open to the world than she could have imagined.

Although Betty has been gone for nearly fifteen years, there are still many things I want to tell her. That, as she predicted, when I began to write about the sad state of devotional verse and the vapid language of contemporary hymns, I often found myself speaking to deaf ears. She cautioned me to recognize that "most people interpret the word 'poetry' to mean a sentimental, soft view of the world, and need a renewed sense of language to see the depth and severity of poetry." This had been her life's work. I long to tell her of the provocative things that contemporary scholarship has uncovered in

Scripture, for example, that Jesus' words "The kingdom of God is within you" in the New Revised Standard Version are an alternative translation: a more accurate rendering is "The Kingdom of God is *among* you," which would have pleased Betty, confirming her sense of community as the essential of human life.

In our final conversation, Betty seemed to take solace in knowing I was well settled in my marriage, and in the town to which I had moved at twenty-seven. She also was glad that my flourishing friendships with Benedictine monks and nuns were a new source of inspiration for my life and work. She said to me, "I like the person you're becoming." Her words were not a confirmation but a challenge. And a blessing, acknowledging that while I had been remarkably immature when she met me, she now thought that I might amount to something, after all. But it remains an open question, and the blessing holds only as long as I keep asking whether the person I am is, in this moment, someone Betty would want to befriend. I know now that God works with us as we are, and through other people becomes incarnate to us. When I pray Psalm 25, "Do not remember the sins of my youth, but in your love remember me," it is Betty's vigilant, vigorous, and loyal love that I think of, as I give thanks to God.

ELIZABETH KRAY

ACKNOWLEDGMENTS

❧

IN WRITING THIS BOOK I HAVE RELIED EXTEN-
sively on the papers that were in Betty Kray's possession at the time
of her death in 1987. I have drawn also from the many interviews I
conducted with poets, arts administrators, philanthropists, and other
friends of Betty Kray, and have cited talks made at her funeral and at
a memorial service. I am deeply indebted to Margo and Anthony
Viscusi, faithful friends of Elizabeth Kray and Vladimir Ussachevsky,
and executors of their estates, for their patience with me in the years
it took to put this book together.

I owe the poet laureate of the United States, Stanley Kunitz, a
special debt of gratitude, not only for more than three decades of
support for every poetry project that Betty Kray dreamed up, but
also for giving me a lengthy and extraordinarily helpful interview in

1991. Memoirs by Donald Hall, Harvey Shapiro, Louis Simpson, and Larry Woiwode have been of use, and also Phillip Lopate's *Journal of a Living Experiment*, a history of the first ten years of the Teachers & Writers Collaborative, and *The World Is Flippied and Damzled About*, a long-out-of-print book commissioned by the Ohio Arts Council that provided Betty Kray with her only public opportunity to tell the story of her pilot program that first sent poets into American classrooms.

I owe thanks to the institutions for which Betty worked, and to individuals who helped me with my research, notably Mrs. James A. Wright and the staff of Poets House, especially Molly Dempsey; and Steven W. Siegel, library director and archivist at the 92nd Street Y, and William Wadsworth, executive director of the Academy of American Poets, whose hospitality and generosity went far beyond the call of duty. I gratefully acknowledge their permission to reprint excerpts from Betty's letters.

I appreciate the friendship and support of Lynn, Susan, Cindy, and Erin; and the diligent attention Anna gave to the manuscript.

I am aware, as Czeslaw Milosz has written, that "the past is inaccurate." Both personal and institutional memories grow dim over time, and it is not easy to reconstruct an era, and a life, even if it is one's own. I have done all I can to ensure accuracy in this book, and can only hope that the errors that remain will not cause anyone harm.

PERMISSIONS

I thank June Jordan, Cynthia Macdonald, Gerard Malanga, Carol Muske, Gregory Orr, and Mrs. James A. Wright for allowing me to reprint personal correspondence, and gratefully acknowledge permission to quote from the following:

Meredith Carson, "Micro," from *Infinite Morning,* copyright 1997 by Meredith Carson. Reprinted by permission of Ohio University Press.

John Haines, "The Sweater of Vladimir Ussachevsky," from *News from the Glacier: Selected Poems 1960–1980,* copyright 1982 by John Haines, Wesleyan University Press. Reprinted by permission of University Press of New England.